To: Rachael Smith

PRAYBOOK

"It is my prayer that this book will not just give you one miracle but the knowledge and understanding you get from here will help you record several victories from prayer"

— Olamide

PRAY BOOK

BIBLICAL STRATEGY FOR BUILDING A PRAYER LIFE

xxxxxxxx

EMMANUEL IREN

PRAY BOOK

ISBN: 978-978-784-896-8

Copyright 2023 Emmanuel Iren

All rights reserved. No portion of this publication may be reproduced by any means without permission of the publisher, the only exception being the pages specified which can be copied in sufficient quantity for use in a mentoring program but not for sale.

All Scripture passages are taken from the Holy Bible, King James Version and the New King James Version, except otherwise stated.

For more information, contact:
Email – emmanuelirenassist@gmail.com

Cover Design by Abraham *Ajay Whisper* Junaid
Layout by Shobola Ibukun

Introduction / **v**

Chapter One
Who Is Asking? / **1**

Chapter Two
Abba, the Trainer Dad / **13**

Chapter Three
When I Don't Feel Close to God / **24**

Chapter Four
Provoked! (Corporate Prayer) / **32**

Chapter Five
Private Prayer Time / **45**

Chapter Six
How to Pray (Priorities In Prayer) / **64**

Chapter Seven
How Not To Pray / **83**

Chapter Eight
Fervency in Prayer / **89**

Chapter Nine
Runaway Knocks / **102**

Chapter Ten
Hypertrophy in Prayer | *112*

Chapter Eleven
Tongues Part 1: Why, What, and Whom | *120*

Chapter Twelve
Tongues Part 2: How to Speak in Tongues | *146*

Chapter Thirteen
Gaining Back Spiritual Form | *158*

Chapter Fourteen
A Final Guide to Prayer | *167*

INTRODUCTION

xxxxxxxx

For most of my primary school years, I thought I was an average student. But my life changed when we moved houses, and I had to change schools. At this new school, the teacher was quite committed to our growth. And just like that, my life began to change. I ended up having one of the highest school leaving scores in the country. Before you think me to be some genius, remember that this was primary school. The transformation meant a lot to me nonetheless. What was even more phenomenal was that the poorest score in my class was 402/600. It proved to me that almost all the time, we are one good teacher away from being the best version of ourselves.

I believe that this book will be to you what that teacher was to me. Have you ever felt bad about your prayer life? I mean, you know you ought to pray but somehow you don't. Perhaps that's why you are reading this book. Well, I have good news for you. It doesn't matter how bad your prayer life currently is; you can do better, and I am optimistic you will. Maybe five minutes of prayer seems like five days. Or it seems like the heaven over you is shut and no one is listening. You are one good book away from revitalising your prayer life.

This book will also be helpful to people who already have a prayer life but seek to do better, or at least understand the doctrine of prayer better. Wherever you are in your journey, I welcome you to the School of Prayer. The Bible says in 2 Timothy 3:16 that "All scripture *is* given by inspiration of God, and *is* profitable for doctrine, for reproof, for correction, for instruction in righteousness."

A synonym for the word translated as *instruction* here is 'tutelage' (or education). Meaning every child of God should be enrolled in the school of the Word. The particular subject we will be studying in this school is prayer. There is a school of prayer. It is for this reason that the disciples of Jesus could say to Him: "Teach us to pray." (Luke 11:1) You can learn to pray. You can build the discipline of prayer only by learning and exercise.

Introduction

By the way, the teaching is not only for novices. The disciples of Jesus, being Jews and (some of them) former disciples of John, knew how to pray. How did they know that "John taught his disciples to pray"? Because they used to be John's disciples. If anything, being Jews, they came from a rich heritage of prayer. They had the Psalms of David, the Lamentations of Jeremiah, and the entire scriptures, which they most probably read religiously. But the day the disciples saw Jesus pray, they knew they had a lot to learn! That's where some of you are. You are reading this book because God put a hunger in your heart for more. You want to pray and see power. You are tired of playing church.

I am even more keen on helping the beginners. The ones who are struggling to even keep a consistent prayer watch. I have called this book **PRAYBOOK**, just like the playbook coaches use to draw strategies for their teams to excel on the court or field. I want to help you curate a strategy for a consistent prayer life. I cannot wait to hear your testimonies!

CHAPTER ONE

WHO IS ASKING?

×××××××

The average height in the NBA is six foot five. Meaning that no matter how hard you work, the likelihood of you playing in the NBA begins with something outside your control—your height. Don't get it wrong, no one can become an NBA player without hard work. It is about the most competitive league and the hardest to get into. Amongst many other reasons this is so, there are only about 500 players in the entire league, and the whole world literally has to fight for one of those 500 spots. I said all of this to emphasise the place of effort. Yet, in spite of how hard you may be willing to work, grace plays a major factor in all of this. If you are not tall, you almost certainly cannot compete at that level.

Statistically, anyone who is six foot three is taller than 95 percent of the rest of the world. But a person of that height is considered short in the NBA. Like many other aspects of life, making it into the NBA has much to do with *being* than *doing*. Yes, what you do has a lot to do with it. You'd need to train hard every day, with the right coach and diet. But at the end of the day, height is necessary and it is a gift.

What if I told you that the most important aspect of prayer is not in the doing but in the being? Let me paint you a scenario. If you were walking on the street and a random person came to you to request two hundred dollars, what would you do? Like most people, you might respectfully say: "Sorry, I cannot give you that." Mind you, you may even be on your way to spend more than that, so your refusal wasn't based on capacity, but on trust and commitment. Simply put, you don't know or trust the stranger enough to grant such a request. However, I am sure that there are people in your life who, if they came to you with the same request, even if you didn't have it to give, you would do everything within your power to ensure they got help somehow. What makes the difference? The way the question is asked, or who is asking? Definitely the latter! This, my friend, is the first thing to know about prayer. It is not first and foremost about making the right prayer requests, the fervour with which you prayed, or even calling the undoubtedly powerful name of Jesus. It is first about who you are in the sight of God. The mere privilege and audacity to call to God must never be overlooked.

This book in your hands is probably the latest of a few other books on prayer that you've already read. The average believer has either read or at least heard in sermons, a myriad of teachings on prayer, emphasising different perspectives and strategies for an effective prayer life. But sometimes, we get the most important thing wrong by focusing on just the prayer requests and better 'techniques' for making them. But I painted that scenario to help you see that the wrong person can almost never say the right things. Likewise, prayer is first about *who* is talking before it is about *what* the person talking is saying. So again, before we talk about quiet times, prayer postures, praying in faith, and other things you probably expect to learn about, my first urgent question to you is who are you?

The Right to Stand Before God

There is almost no book on prayer that doesn't use **James 5:16b** as one of its proof texts. This verse says: "The effective, fervent prayer of a righteous man avails much." There is a plethora of sermons drawing from this text, the importance of fervour and/or importunity in prayer. All of this will be discussed later on in this book; however, we almost always leave out what I argue to be the most important detail in **James 5:16b**. The text doesn't just tell us how to pray to get results, it also tells us who prays. The effectual fervent prayer of a RIGHTEOUS man. Again, it all boils down to who you are.

What is righteousness? It is the ability to stand before God without guilt or shame. It is the audacity with which we "come boldly" before the throne of grace **(Hebrews 4:16)**. Righteousness is a serious matter in prayer because the prayer of the wicked is an abomination to the Lord **(Proverbs 15:8, 28:9)**. The prophet Isaiah says: "Behold, the LORD's hand is not shortened, that it cannot save; nor His ear heavy, that it cannot hear. But your iniquities have separated you from your God;, and your sins have hid *His* face from you, so that He will not hear." **(Isaiah 59:1-2)**

Unfortunately, there isn't a single one of us good enough in and of ourselves. The Bible says in **Romans 3:23**, "For all have sinned and fall short of the glory of God." There is not a single one of us for whom Jesus did not need to die. Before a thrice holy God, even the best of us will not be good enough by our personal merits or righteousness. Isaiah lets us know that "all our righteousnesses are like filthy rags" **(Isaiah 64:6)**. By our own works of righteousness, we could never measure up to God's standards. If we would ever be righteous before God, it would first be a gift of grace before a walk. Bear in mind that the fact

WHO IS ASKING?

that our efforts will never be enough does not mean they are not required. Just the same way a tall person would still have to learn to bounce the ball to play in the NBA. Like height is a gift that was not earned by the NBA player, righteousness is a gift to the believer **(Romans 5:17)**.

The good news is that God sent Jesus to take our place, die for our sins, and bequeath to us His own righteousness. Now, in the place of prayer, the believer stands as though Christ Himself in His righteousness were the one making the request. The Bible says: "For He made Him who knew no sin to be sin for us, that we might become the righteousness of God in Him." **(1 Corinthians 5:21)**

This righteousness changes everything! This righteousness is what makes our effectual and fervent prayer count. This is because prayer is designed to be a spiritual family affair. A discussion between the Father and His children. Your confidence in the place of prayer should stem from the assurance of your identity. Who are you?

A story in the book of Acts perfectly portrays an example of all I have been saying. Luke tells us of the sons of Sceva. They had taken notes on Paul's style of prayer and casting out demons. Just like many people, these men thought it was about the tone of voice, the hand gestures and posture, or even mentioning the name of Jesus. The Bible says: "Then some of the itinerant Jewish exorcists took it upon themselves to call the name of the Lord Jesus over those who had evil spirits, saying, 'We exorcise you by the Jesus whom Paul preaches.' Also there were seven sons of Sceva, a Jewish chief priest, who did so. And the evil spirit answered and said, 'Jesus I know, and Paul I know; but who are you?'" **(Acts 19:13-15)**

The question, "Who are you?" is a question of identity. These men wanted to replicate the result they had seen in the life of Paul. However, they did not have the same identity that Paul had. Their intention was to commit spiritual identity theft. They were not saved, yet they wanted to use the name of Jesus. The Bible lets us know that it didn't quite end well for them: "Then the man in whom the evil spirit was leaped on them, overpowered them, and prevailed against them, so that they fled out of that house naked and wounded." **(Acts 19:16)**

This goes to show that prayer is not just about the words you say, but it is also fundamentally about who you are. The sons of Sceva wanted to act out who they weren't. It is amusing that there are people who don't want Jesus but want what Jesus can do.

Pray for Me

The real objective of this chapter is to address two classes of people. The first class are believers who are yet to understand how the sheer privilege of being in Christ gives them access and authority in prayer. The second class are those who are not born again but like to pray. Oh yes, there are people like that; do not feel judged if you are one of them. For some, like Cornelius, they never heard the gospel, but know there is a God and pray to Him **(Acts 10:1-2)**. For others, like the multitude in Jesus' day, they trust God only for miracles, but do not believe in Him or live a life that honours Him.

Anyone who does a bit of evangelism knows that most people do not mind being prayed for. Not only do they not mind, they'd readily ask for it. I'll never forget my experience at a bus stop somewhere in Mushin, Lagos. Some thugs heard someone call me *pastor*, and they immediately came to me for prayers. Heads bowed, eyes shut, with marijuana hanging from their mouths. They asked me to pray that God would bless them and help their businesses. They believed that God could do that and trusted Him to do it. But the moment I tried to preach to them about salvation, their countenances visibly changed. They were not interested. They wanted what God could do but they did not want God.

Does God hear the prayers of sinners? He sure does. But the reason for His goodness is to challenge them to deeper levels of spiritual commitment as His children. God performed a myriad of incredible miracles in Egypt to deliver the Israelites even though they were in unbelief. God is that good! You may be seeing that in your life. Perhaps you haven't paid God any attention yet He keeps blessing you. Friend, that's like a man at the talking stage with a woman. It would be irresponsible of her to keep going on dates, receiving gifts with no plans to move the relationship forward. At some point, even the most patient man should ask, "What are we?" Likewise, God wants a relationship with you! If you are not born again, you must be born again. If you are born again but have no walk with God, it's time to wake up! God asked me to use the first chapter of this book to challenge you. If you are a believer who hasn't taken his/her walk with God seriously lately, it's time to wake up!

Do you realise that this is why after several miracles and after crossing the Red Sea, God stops the children of Israel at Sinai to define the relationship (by giving them the law). As though to say, "No more free rides. Commit before you continue."

You know what's funny? Even from a selfish standpoint, many are so shallow. Why would anyone rather choose to receive occasional handouts from a wealthy man instead of being his son? His son is heir of all things! Prayer is a business of relationship. It is meant to be a family matter. However, some have insisted on being strangers. Do they not know that the powers and potentialities of prayer move to a whole new dimension when the basis of your relationship with God changes? Again I ask, who are you?

Stand in Righteousness

Let me bring this text back to you: **James 5:16b** – "The effectual fervent prayer of a righteous man availeth much." This means that righteousness is a consciousness in prayer. The believer in Christ must learn to say:

> **I am made righteous by the grace of God. Jesus died for me and rose again on the third day. I have received all that Jesus did. I have received the Holy Spirit. I have ACCESS to the Father. This is my consciousness in the place of prayer. If I have received the righteousness of Jesus, it means that God loves me as much as He loves Jesus. Therefore, I am forever a winner in the place of prayer! Amen.**

Take a break to say these words and watch your soul get stirred. See, there may be a million things I am yet to learn about prayer, but this is the most important I know: God's priority will forever be "Let the children first be filled." **(Mark 7:27)**. This just reveals that identity will always command priority in prayer. This is the identity we are so privileged to have in Christ! Every time you get to pray, be confident in that identity. Like Jesus, you can say, *"Father, I thank you that you hear me always."* **(John 11:41-42)**.

It will change your prayer life if, instead of wondering if your prayers cross the ceiling, you **know** that you always have access to the Father in prayer. John says, "And this is the confidence that we have in him, that, if we ask anything according to his will, he heareth us:" **(1 John 5:14)** Be confident in prayer! You are the righteousness of God in Christ. Hallelujah.

Action Steps

What do you do when you wake up in the morning and it seems like your prayers are not getting beyond the ceiling? With these powerful confessions and verses of scripture, you can stir yourself up. Repeat each point as often as five times.

1. **Ephesians 1:3-4** – "Blessed *be* the God and Father of our Lord Jesus Christ, who has blessed us with every spiritual blessing in the heavenly *places* in Christ, just as He chose us in Him before the foundation of the world, that we should be holy and without blame before Him in love."
   Prayer/Confession – Lord, I thank you that I am blessed

with every spiritual blessing in the heavenly places in Christ. Before the foundation of the world, you chose me in Christ to be holy and blameless. Therefore, I rejoice that I have access! You are not far from me!

2. **Ephesians 1:7** – "In Him we have redemption through His blood, the forgiveness of sins, according to the riches of His grace."
   Prayer/Confession- I confess that in Christ, I have redemption. In Christ I have forgiveness.

3. **2 Corinthians 5:21** – "For He made Him who knew no sin *to be* sin for us, that we might become the righteousness of God in Him."
   Prayer/Confession – I am the righteousness of God in Christ Jesus.

4. **Romans 5:1-2** – "Therefore, having been justified by faith, [a]we have peace with God through our Lord Jesus Christ, through whom also we have access by faith into this grace in which we stand, and rejoice in hope of the glory of God."
   Prayer/Confession – I have been justified by faith in Jesus Christ. Now I have peace with God. I have access to God. I stand by faith in what Christ has done. I rejoice in the hope of the Glory of God.

5. **Romans 8:14-15** – "For as many as are led by the Spirit of God, these are sons of God. For you did not receive the spirit of bondage again to fear, but you received the Spirit of adoption by whom we cry out, 'Abba, Father.'"

   Prayer/Confession – I have the Spirit of God. I have the Spirit of adoption. I am led by the Spirit. God is my Father. God is my Daddy. He hears me when I pray. I can boldly call him Father.

For the sake of this book, I will stop at these five. Here's a second exercise:

– Read through the epistles. Identify verses that tell you about your righteousness and access to God. Write them down and pray them over yourself consistently.

CHAPTER TWO

ABBA, THE TRAINER DAD

x x x x x x x x

As a flow of thought from the previous chapter that asked and answered the question, "Who are you?," let's now answer the question, "Who is God?"

An inconsistent prayer life is often a result of a low view of God. How invested do you think God is in your growth? If you are reading this book as one who is a beginner in the business of prayer, or one who has tried and failed to develop a consistent prayer life, receiving God as your Father and trainer is a good place to start.

Your biological parents have trained you and raised you, and remain committed to you unconditionally. Your boss, however, only cares about deliverables. You either get the job done or you are shown the way out. Your relationship with your boss at work is based on performance. Sadly, many Christians treat God like He is merely their boss. They probably picture prayer like work hours that they must clock in. I'm a firm believer in proper investment of time in the place of prayer, but there is more to your relationship with God than that!

The only basis of a boss' relationship with the employee is performance. But if the boss should choose to discontinue the employee's contract, guess where the employee goes? Home to his/her family. This is because even if every father, mother, or sibling expects us to do well, their acceptance of us is not based on our performance. The biological father is expected to train and correct his wards. Our heavenly Father is no different. He isn't watching to see if you finally get this prayer thing together or He kicks you out. He is for you! He will teach you to pray. He will guide your devotional development. Make no mistake, He will correct you sternly when He needs to, but He will never give up on you. That's your Daddy!

Why is this important? It is important because the devil haunts people with the fact that they tried to pray and failed. Make no mistake, there is no excuse for not having a prayer life. If I thought there was one, I wouldn't write a whole book on prayer. But letting the devil use that to make you give up is counterproductive. Let Daddy help you pray!

The Fatherhood of God in Prayer

So, who is God, really? The most radical change that has happened in the New Testament is the Fatherhood of God to the believer. The Bible tells us that the disciples of Jesus asked that He teach them to pray, and He taught them to pray thus: *"Our Father"* (**Luke 11:2**). The revelation of the Fatherhood of God to the believer is foundational to effective prayer in the New Testament. In **Romans 8:15**, the Bible says: "For you did not receive the spirit of bondage again to fear, but you received the Spirit of adoption by whom we cry out, 'Abba, Father.'"

From the text above, you should see why this is important to our discourse on prayer. In prayer, we must know that the one to whom we 'cry' is Father. The one to whom we cry (or pray) is as important as what we cry. The revelation of sonship influences our prayer life. We cry differently. Not as slaves or mere employees, but as sons.

God is Alpha and Omega; beginning and end. He is all this and more, but what a privilege it is to call Him Daddy! Whatever it is you need; a supernatural intervention, a healing, or just intimacy, understand that God is your Daddy! The Holy Spirit is the spirit of adoption. That is, the Spirit of sonship. What this simply means is that by being born again and receiving the Holy Spirit, you become a son of God. God becomes your Daddy. The God of the whole universe is your Daddy now. Friend, this ought to radically change your perspective in prayer.

Two Implications of the Fatherhood of God

1. **ACCESS:**

    You may have seen a great man before. Perhaps someone with a robust entourage and several layers of bureaucracy before you can get access. But in normal cases, if that person has a child, all those protocols don't apply to that child. Especially where the matter is of an urgent nature, the child can simply walk into the office, past all the security officials and protocols, past all the queues of people waiting to see their 'boss', and straight into daddy's office. When daddy looks at his child's face, he could ask all his staff to excuse them immediately; "I need a few minutes to talk to my child. Everything else has to wait."

    This paints a vivid picture of what it means that God is Abba to us. By the way, people loosely translate Abba to mean Daddy. But a more literal translation of the word used in Romans 8:15 will be the more informal word "Dada." It is the cry of a baby that is more informal, less articulate, and reflects endearment. When a child is learning to talk, he or she does not need to call out daddy articulately to get their father's attention. Anything sincere works! The sound of the child will always command the attention of the father.

This is not a call for you to be nonchalant in prayer, or to not care to pray in the biblically prescribed way. This is to let you know that ultimately, God is not looking for technical perfection. He will not despise a broken and contrite heart!

Another reason this is important is that the devil plagues with guilt the minds of people who haven't prayed in a while. To be clear, if you haven't prayed in a while, you should feel guilty. Very guilty. But that guilt should come from your conscience and from the nudge of the Spirit. Some people even stand in the place of prayer obsessing about the fact that they have not prayed in a while instead of actually praying. That's counterproductive and sometimes, even an attack of the devil. It will help you to remember that even the prodigal son is always welcome back home! Never forget that.

2. VULNERABILITY:

A lot of believers still cannot wrap their minds around the fact that in the Garden of Gethsemane, Jesus prayed thus:

"If it is possible, let this cup pass over me." Did Jesus really mean those words? Absolutely! Jesus prayed with no filters! As overwhelming as His love for us was, He thought about the scourging and the crucifixion, and in a moment of vulnerability, asked: "Is there any other way?"

The problem is that some people pray to prove how strong and disciplined they are, instead of praying to draw strength. What if we learnt to talk to God honestly about how we feel? You are struggling in your prayer life? Pray about it. Are you overwhelmed with temptations? Pray about it. The Fatherhood of God helps you realise you can be real with God.

Why Are You Sleeping?

We don't learn vulnerability only from Jesus at Gethsemane, we also learn about the vulnerability of his disciples. Bear in mind that this was one of the most vulnerable moments of Jesus' earthly ministry. He knew the time had come to face the cross, and that it was not going to be easy. "My soul is exceeding sorrowful unto death," He said **(Matthew 26:38)**. The pressure really told on Him. This was why Jesus had come to that garden to pray. He desperately needed to! At that crucial time, He wasn't going to invite all His disciples to be with Him; He invited only the three closest ones: Peter, James, and John—all who should have recognised the enormity of the privilege. These ones had the honour and privilege to watch with Jesus. But what did they do? They went there and slept off!

Have you ever tried to pray and then slept off? Well, Jesus' disciples have been there. This should encourage you, that if they struggled with sleep but still went ahead to build a formidable devotional life and accomplish all that God would have them accomplish as apostles, so can you!

As a pastor, I learnt a huge lesson on how to teach with grace and patience from Jesus' response. Just imagine, on a lighter note, that you went to the prayer room with a top man of God today and slept off. How do you suppose that would have turned out? I asked this because some people seem to think that they can ridicule others into spiritual fervour. However, that wasn't Jesus' approach. I can't get over His humility in waking up Peter to pray. Jesus didn't say, "Get out of here, since you are not willing to pray with me at this crucial time." He sure didn't fail to warn them of the consequences of not praying either. Jesus said: "If you do not pray, you will fall into temptation." Yet, three times, He patiently woke them up, saying, "The Spirit is willing but the flesh is weak." It is this kind of balance that a teaching on devotions requires.

It is life-changing, however, that God is not waiting for you to either pray or get lost. God is on your side. He is a trainer. He is empathetic. While He won't pamper you in your laziness as though it didn't matter, He won't give up on you either.

It Is God

The text I'm about to share with you is the most profound when it comes to building Christian devotions in any area. The text says:

> *"For it is God who works in you both to will and to do for His good pleasure."*
> **- Philippians 2:13**

If you receive this truth, it will change your life! Friend, the mere realisation that you need to pray more is proof that God is at work in you. The fact that you have this book in your hands and have read up until this point is proof that God is at work in you. "The will to do" is a miracle. It is God who does that!

Forever etched in my memory is the funny, fictional but powerful story of an unusual friendship between an elephant and an ant. These two went out for an evening walk and crossed a wooden bridge. As you could expect, the bridge shook with each step the elephant took. Having gotten to the other side successfully, the ant looked at the elephant and said, "We shook that bridge, didn't we?" This is the picture of the devotional life of every believer. On one hand, there is absolutely no way to build a consistent devotional life without effort and discipline. But the words of Jesus must resound in our consciousness thus: *"For without Me, you can do nothing."* **(John 15:5)**

In other words, God is on your side! You can only truly excel at devotions in partnership with God who works in YOU, to WILL and to DO His good pleasure. You know, you might even be ashamed of yourself right now for how bad your prayer life is. You may have cried to God for help in your prayer life. But the mere realisation that you need help is proof that God is already working in you. In case you didn't know, Paul says that IT IS GOD who works in you, so that you WILL and DO His good pleasure. The desire to pray is of God, and praying is of God as well.

Learning to trust this is a great first step, but that's not the only step. Don't stop and simply say, "Well, at least I desire to pray. I'm not doing too bad." No. Paul says that the realisation that God is working in you to will and do should push you to "work out your salvation." The true working of God will not remain a secret. If

God is working IN you, you will work OUT your salvation. This simply means that sooner than later, we must begin to see in your devotions, the evidence of the work of the Spirit. If you no longer even care much about your poor prayer life, that's something to act on urgently. It is good that such a person is reading this.

Action Steps

> *"As His divine power has given to us all things that pertain to life and godliness, through the knowledge of Him who called us by glory and virtue, by which have been given to us exceedingly great and precious promises, that through these you may be partakers of the divine nature, having escaped the corruption that is in the world through lust."*
>
> **- 2 Peter 1:3-4**

In this chapter, emphasis was placed on God's role as our Father and trainer, as it relates to prayer. For your next action step, I want you to consciously acknowledge this in the place of prayer. Are you struggling with your prayer life, pray about it. Remember: a broken and contrite heart, He will not despise. Pray these:rd, I thank You that all that I need for life and godliness, I already have by the Spirit. All that I need to have a consistent prayer life is on my inside. I have escaped the corruption and distractions of this world. I have a divine nature. I can have a fervent devotional life aided by the Spirit of God. Father, I submit myself to your training in my prayer life, in Jesus name. I yield to the help of your Spirit. Let the giant in me arise, and let mediocrity die, in Jesus name. Father, I know that the will to 'do' comes from you. I therefore declare that I am a doer of your Word today. I obey, even when I don't feel like it. I obey, even when it is not convenient. I obey you without reservation. In Jesus name.

CHAPTER THREE
WHEN I DON'T FEEL CLOSE TO GOD

✗ ✗ ✗ ✗ ✗ ✗ ✗ ✗

No matter what you read in this book or in any other, if you do not learn what I'm about to show you, you will still have struggles in your walk with God. One of the biggest secrets to vibrant devotions is this:

> *"For we walk by faith, not by sight."*
> **2 Corinthians 5:7**

So, you woke up in the morning and you prayed, but it seemed like God didn't hear you. Who told you so? You prayed and did not feel close to God. Who told you so? You will continue to be a prisoner of your feelings until you learn to walk by faith and not by sight! Growing up spiritually requires that you know to see with more than just your eyes, hear with more than just your ears, and touch with more than just your hands. This is the very basis of your salvation and your relationship with God in general. About God, the Bible says in **1 Peter 1:8**: "Whom having not seen you love. Though now you do not see Him, yet believing, you rejoice with joy inexpressible and full of glory."

Maybe no one ever spelt it out for you: **you are in a relationship with a God you have never seen!** The most authentic love you have ever felt is with and to a God you have never seen. The natural man may call it foolish, but this is the biggest love story ever told. Apostle Peter says, "Though now you do not see Him, yet believing, you rejoice with joy inexpressible and full of glory." We believe and we rejoice! This joy is not a feeling but a knowing! This is the bedrock of a vibrant spiritual experience.

Let me surprise you now. Do you know that, strictly speaking, we cannot call ourselves witnesses of Christ? Don't get me wrong, we are witnesses, but not in the exact context of Acts 1:8 where Christ said, *"You shall be witnesses unto me..."* To be a witness is to see, hear, or know by personal presence or perception. Jesus called His disciples 'witnesses' because they saw the risen Christ; Quite unlike us, of whom Peter said: "Though we see Him not, believe."

You see, the disciples came to believe, having seen indisputable evidence. Many believers read **Acts 1:8** but not the preceding verses. Follow the train of thought from **Acts 1:1-3**:

> 1 "The former treatise have I made, O Theophilus, of all that Jesus began both to do and teach, 2 until the day in which he was taken up, after that he through the Holy Ghost had given commandments unto the apostles whom he had chosen: 3 to whom also he shewed himself alive after his passion by many infallible proofs, being seen of them forty days, and speaking of the things pertaining to the kingdom of God:"

Jesus showed Himself alive to the disciples with many infallible proofs. He lived with them 40 full days. That's long enough for any hallucination to wear off, had it been one. But they were not dreaming; Jesus was indeed alive! Even when the disciple some mockingly call The Doubting Thomas said, *"Except I shall see in his hands the print of the nails, and put my finger into the print of the nails, and thrust my hand into his side, I will not believe."* **(John 20:25)**. He wanted nothing but evidence, and he still got it. Jesus appeared to Thomas and said: *"...Reach your finger here, and look at My hands; and reach your hand here, and put it into My side. Do not be unbelieving, but believing."* **- John 20:27**

When Thomas touched Jesus, his doubt went out the window. It was true; it is true. Jesus is alive! In awe and worship, the Bible says: *"And Thomas answered and said to Him, 'My Lord and my God!'"* **- John 20:28**

There is a huge lesson to learn from Jesus' response. Follow closely and read this powerful verse: *"Jesus said to him, 'Thomas, because you have seen Me, you have believed. Blessed are those who have not seen and yet have believed.'"* **- John 20:29**

Blessed are those who haven't seen but believe! He was talking about you and me!

I Saw Jesus

You may have read testimonies of people who claim to have seen Jesus appear to them. Some of them may be true and many of them false, but sometimes, you might hear such stories and think, "God must truly love them. I wonder when He will appear to me." Look, thank God for supernatural encounters; I do not in any way downplay them. However, Jesus said: "Blessed are those, who have not seen but believe!"

Now to your prayer life. Since when did feelings become the yardstick for discerning spirituality? Do you not know that your feelings are often a bad judge? Do you not realise that you can be great in the sight of God and not know it? You can be dearly loved by the Father and not accept it because you do not "feel" so? Think about what Angel Gabriel said to Mary:

> *"And the angel came in unto her, and said, Hail, thou that art highly favoured, the Lord is with thee: blessed art thou among women. And when she saw him, she was troubled at his saying, and cast in her mind what manner of salutation this should be."*
> **Luke 1:28-29**

Mary was highly favoured and didn't know until the angel of God said so! His salutation even startled her! Far too many Christians need to wake up from their slumber to realise the Lord has been with them all along and they did not know it. Like Jacob in **Genesis 28:16**, wake up from your sleep and see that God is with you! You are not alone.

The Prodigal Son

Do you know why it took so long for the prodigal son to return? It was because he was sure that his father no longer saw him as a son. How could he, after all the boy had done? The prodigal son felt his father no longer wanted him, but guess what? He was wrong! You can feel far from God yet not be. Those boring seasons of devotions might in actuality be some of the most significant in the realm of the Spirit. The problem is that most times, we are looking for God in the wrong places. We expect drama. We expect God to put up a show. Oh, how wrong we are! Let's learn from Elijah's encounter in **1 Kings 19:11-12**:

> *"And he said, Go forth, and stand upon the mount before the LORD. And, behold, the LORD passed by, and a great and strong wind rent the mountains, and brake in pieces the rocks before the LORD; but the LORD was not in the wind: and after the wind an earthquake; but the LORD was not in the earthquake: and after the earthquake a fire; but the LORD was not in the fire: and after the fire a still small voice."*

Stop looking for theatrics! Embrace the simple Word of God. I hope that the text you are about to read changes your life as it did mine!

> *"But without faith it is impossible to please him: for he that cometh to God must believe that he is, and that he is a rewarder of them that diligently seek him."*
> **Hebrews 11:6**

Gosh! God is not a rewarder only when you feel He is. He is a rewarder, period! It is either this text is a lie or some of our experiences are exaggerated or even outright lies. But we know already that God's Word is always true. Sometimes, we might pray and it seems like we got nothing because we *felt* nothing, but on the strength and integrity of the Word of God, we ought to know that prayer will NEVER be a waste of time. You have never sincerely prayed a prayer that God didn't hear. He is a rewarder of those who diligently seek Him! Hallelujah!

Therefore, the best way to have a vibrant walk with God is to walk by faith and not by sight! Let your feelings catch up. Prayer will never be a waste of time. This is a mindset you ought to maintain every time you pray. That "I come to God, knowing that He is a rewarder. He has not called the seed of Jacob to seek Him in vain; therefore, I animate my praise and worship, whether I feel like it or not, and my feelings will catch up! I don't wait to see how I feel—I tell myself how to feel. I engage in self-talk like David and say, 'Bless the Lord, O my soul.' I command my desires and affections; they do not command me." This is how to command and direct your feelings.

Now, one important point to note is that sometimes, your feelings might be a pointer to something you haven't been doing right. If you have been in sin, for example, you should feel bad about that, unless you are reprobate. But even then, do not stay down! Repent and do not allow the devil to sell to you the counterproductive idea of shying away from prayer because you have transgressed. That's like a sick person running away from the doctor because he/she feels too sick. Remember the story of the prodigal son? Your Father's arms are always open.

So, engage in self-talk when you feel down. Remind yourself of who you are in the Lord. Walk by faith and not by sight, knowing that your prayers will never be a waste of time.

Action Steps

Say this when you do not feel close to God:

Dear Jesus, I thank you for dying for me and rising again on the third day. Having ascended and received of the Father the promised Holy Spirit, you came into my heart. And so, I am never far from you! You are always in me and for me. Therefore, I declare today that I am full of your Spirit. From the crown of my head to the soles of my feet and tips of my toes. I am full of you! When I feel it, and when I don't; I know it, still! I am full of you forever! Glory!

CHAPTER FOUR
PROVOKED! (CORPORATE PRAYER)

x x x x x x x x

The popular saying, "there is safety in numbers" fully comes to life in nature with animals largely considered as prey. It has been proven that zebras, antelopes, and other animals in this category move and graze in a herd because it makes it more difficult for predatory animals to attack them. In fact, the herd strategy is so powerful, a confusion of stampeding wildebeest can trample a lion to death.

For the zebras especially, the combination of their stripes and the herd strategy provide a sort of illusion that makes it difficult for the predator to identify a single one of them to attack. However, if one zebra strays from the herd, it is easily stalked and promptly killed by a predator. So, for the safety of any individual zebra, it must stay with the herd.

Just like the security of the zebra lies in staying with the herd, the safety of the believer is in fellowshiping with the church. The church is God's system for our growth. The church is God's strategy for our safety. **Hebrews 10:24-25** says:

> *"And let us consider how we may spur one another on toward love and good deeds, not giving up meeting together, as some are in the habit of doing, but encouraging one another—and all the more as you see the Day approaching."*

There is a modern-day individualistic brand of Christianity that is foreign to the scriptures. Under ideal circumstances, you are not supposed to do it on your own. It is not entirely strange that a growing Christian needs help maintaining a consistent prayer life. A beginner's prayer life is built in community. The Bible says:

> *"We then who are strong ought to bear with the scruples of the weak, and not to please ourselves. Let each of us please his neighbour for his good, leading to edification. For even Christ did not please Himself; but as it is written, 'The reproaches of those who reproached You fell on Me.'"*
> **Romans 15:1-3 NKJV**

From a natural standpoint, there is the temptation to simply conclude that some people are prayerful and others aren't, and that's that. Yet, God's idea is that those who excel should help those who struggle. We are called the Body of Christ because we are meant to identify with one another and strengthen one another. Paul said the same to the church at Galatia:

> "Brethren, if a man is overtaken in any trespass, you who are spiritual restore such a one in a spirit of gentleness, considering yourself lest you also be tempted."
> **Galatians 6:1 NKJV**

We are meant to help one another. Do you notice that in both instances (Romans & Galatians), Paul mentions that in doing so, we will be following Christ's example? The Christian life is exemplified by selflessness. If you are strong, it's not an occasion to brag; it's an occasion to do ministry. Find someone to help. If you are struggling, stop being ashamed to ask for help. Stop pretending you are doing okay. Reach out for help.

The greatest and most reliable secret of consistent devotions is found in community. Your assembly is meant to contribute to your devotions. The best way to revive your prayer life is not to read a book, although that's a great first step. For a beginner, the best way is to join a community that prays. Your brothers and sisters in Christ have a ministry to you! Receive it.

A General Rule of Life

Any discipline you seek to build is easily built in the right company. Haven't you noticed you struggle to work out on your own, but are motivated when you do it with others? This is exactly why people go to the gym—not just for equipment but for community. What about when you are reading for an exam? Having an accountability partner helps! As a rule of life, whatever you wish to become, you must maintain proximity to. It's the same way you were probably careful to choose friends who were serious with their studies in school, so that you could also stay motivated. Some people also prefer to go to the movies with friends rather than on their own.

It is interesting that many people understand the strength of community and take advantage of it in every aspect of their lives except their walk with God. That's where you hear them say, "Salvation is personal." But there is nothing personal about discipleship. The texts I shared earlier prove that.

The Lord's Prayer Is a Corporate Prayer

Did you ever take notice of the fact that the Lord's prayer is a corporate prayer? I mean, when the disciples asked Jesus to teach them to pray, He taught them to pray thus:

> **Our** Father
> Give **us our** daily bread
> Forgive **us our** trespasses
>
> As **we** forgive those who trespass against **us**

The Lord's Prayer therefore implicitly suggests that we should pray together as often as we can. Listen, private prayer is important and must be encouraged. Yet, here is a secret—especially if you are seeking to build a more consistent private prayer life: use corporate prayer to fan the flames of your private prayer! That is to say, by fellowshipping with prayerful people regularly, your own private altar will be ignited. You will just find yourself praying more than ever before. In fact, one of the simple tests of the health of your prayer life is the frequency of your public prayers. If your soul is healthy as it should be, you'd itch to fellowship with the saints. A simple principle to keep your walk with God sane is to never consistently miss corporate prayer times.

Many other texts both directly and implicitly advocate for accountability, and more specifically, corporate prayer. A few of which are:

- **Colossians 3:16 (NKJV)** – "Let the word of Christ dwell *in* you richly *in* all wisdom, teaching and admonishing <u>one another</u> *in* psalms and hymns and spiritual songs, singing with grace *in* your hearts to the Lord." (Emphasis added)

- **1 Corinthians 14:26 (NKJV)** – "How is it then, brethren? Whenever <u>*you come together*</u>, each of *you* has a psalm, has a teaching, has a tongue, has a revelation, has an interpretation. Let all things be done for edification." (Emphasis added)

- **1 Corinthians 5:4 (NKJV)** – "In the name of our Lord Jesus Christ, <u>*when you* are gathered *together*</u>, along with my spirit, with the power of our Lord Jesus Christ…" (Emphasis added)

- **Ephesians 5:19 (NKJV)** – "<u>Speaking to one another</u> *in* psalms and hymns and spiritual songs, singing and making melody *in* your heart to the Lord." (Emphasis added)

- **Hebrews 10:24-25 (KJV)** – "And let us consider one another to PROVOKE unto love and to good works: not <u>forsaking the assembling of ourselves together</u>, as the manner of some is; but exhorting one another: and so much the more, as ye see the day approaching." (Emphasis added)

Do you want the word of Christ to dwell in you richly? Do you want to overcome that drag in your devotional life? Do you want to be provoked to good works? Then take advantage of fellowship with the saints. Find persons with whom you can teach and admonish in biblical psalms and hymns. Sing together! Worship together. Pray together. This is a game-changer.

The Power of Praying Together

One day, as I prayed, I heard the Lord ask to think about all the times in the Word that people prayed together. I thought through as many as I could: Paul and Silas in prison; the Church praying for Peter's release; the apostles praying in Acts 13; the Hebrew boys in the book of Daniel, and so on. Then the Lord asked me what all those stories had in common.

Then it hit me! Every single time people prayed together in the Bible, something dramatically miraculous happened. That, my friend, is the power of corporate prayers. One shall chase a thousand, and two shall put ten thousand to flight. Our potential increases when we pray together. This is both true regarding power and also devotional discipline. It is the beginners hack to a more effective prayer life. With corporate prayer, two things are likely to happen:

You pray longer

When you are still building a prayer life, you will notice that it is easier to pray longer when praying with people. Accountability and what some may call "corporate anointing" keeps you going. If it were your private prayer time and you planned to pray for an hour, you could stop after twenty minutes if you felt tired. But you are more likely to stick to the plan when you are not alone.

You tend to focus better

Praying with people also helps the beginner focus. Again, it is all about accountability. You are less likely to stop praying and start looking around when others in the room are also praying.

The Hour of Prayer

> *"Now Peter and John went up together to the temple at the hour of prayer, the ninth hour.*
> **- Acts 3:1 NKJV**

Peter and John observed corporate prayer times. According to historical sources, the ninth hour of prayer is around about 3:00 p.m. modern time. Devout Jews observed three times of prayer at the temple—at 9:00 a.m., at noon, and 3:00 p.m. This is also when the morning and evening sacrifices were offered **(Exodus**

29:38-42, Numbers 28:1-8). For the apostles to go to the Temple to pray at these times tells us that they kept the custom at least regarding prayer. This was a corporate hour of prayer, and Peter and John were intent on observing it.

This is a practice you should also adopt. Besides your private prayer time, you should have corporate prayer times. Weekly services are a good place to start. You should do your best to ensure you do not miss that, especially if you are building a prayer life. Some people simply rely on online church services but I assure you, it is not the same. Especially when it comes to being challenged in your devotions. If you have been going to church, then you can take this admonition and resolve to take that fellowship even more seriously. Besides weekly church services, it will also help to have other prayer times. I suggest you have prayer partners. We see a couple of examples of this in the Bible. Let's consider another example:

> "*<u>Now it happened, as we went to prayer,</u> that a certain slave girl possessed with a spirit of divination met us, who brought her masters much profit by fortune-telling. <u>And this she did for many days.</u>*"
> **- Acts 16:16, 18a NKJV** (Emphasis added)

This story tells us that Paul and Silas prayed together regularly. As the text suggests, this lady disturbed them daily on their way to prayer! The Early Church had a rich culture of corporate prayer. Some of us may do better than others without fellowship, but none of us is better without fellowship. You think you're doing okay alone, but you'd be even better with fellowship.

Simple Hacks to Corporate Prayer

1. **Morning devotions:** Some of us grew up in homes where, whether you felt like it or not, family devotions were compulsory. But for varying reasons, that culture died. We must bring that back! No matter how short, you will be shocked at the cumulative impact. The goal is to build the discipline of encouraging one another spiritually in the house.

2. **Attend a praying church:** I cannot stress this enough. No matter how irregular your prayer life is during the week, the right church can jumpstart you every week until you sustain the strength to continue on your own and without fail.

3. **Online prayer platforms:** The advantages of this to a beginner cannot be overemphasised. The argument that online prayers take away people's personal devotions does not apply where many people struggle to pray consistently. Besides, a person who prays well corporately is every bit likely to pray well

privately. The testimonies from the online prayer platform I felt led to institute more than ten years ago is testament. With people tuning in at 6 a.m., noon, 8 p.m., and 2 a.m. (WAT) everyday on YouTube. Triumph30 Devotional has left us with unending testimonies of growth in prayer life. I strongly recommend it or any other platform that works best for you.

4. **Prayer partners:** You know those friends of yours with whom you go to the movies weekly? What if you added a short routine of prayer before you headed out? What if you had a weekly call just to pray? It is life-changing! I know what some of you are thinking. You tried it once before and it died off? Raise another group. If need be, keep raising new groups when the energy of the old one dies off. Whatever be the case, keep on praying!

Provoke One Another

> *"And let us consider one another to **provoke** unto love and to good works: **not forsaking the assembling of ourselves together**, as the manner of some is; **but exhorting one another**: and so much the more, as ye see the day approaching."*
>
> **- Hebrews 10:24-25 KJV** (Emphasis added)

WHEN I DON'T FEEL CLOSE TO GOD

Remember the Lord's Prayer? The disciples saw Jesus' prayer life and were PROVOKED by it. They thought they had a prayer life until they saw Jesus pray. So also must we provoke one another to do good works. The only way to have a vibrant local assembly is when members are actively committed to stirring up one another.

What does the word 'provoke' mean? 'Provoke' is the word *paroxusmos* in Greek. Pronounced par-ox-oos-mos, it means "to incite (to good)", or "dispute (in anger)," "to provoke unto," or "to irritate."

'Paroxusmos' is closely related to another Greek word 'paroxuno', pronounced par-ox-oo-no. Its meanings include "to sharpen/make sharp," "to stimulate," "spur on," or "to urge." It is the word from which the English word "paroxysm" is derived.

From the foregoing paragraph, it is obvious that being "provoked unto good works" is not necessarily a wonderful feeling. Just like how you study more surrounded by friends who do likewise, it might not be a palatable experience, but you still partake in it anyway. Talk about being harassed into doing the right thing. Of course, there are times when we enjoy praying, but perhaps sometimes, our prayers were offered reluctantly to God while thoughts of a movie we watched, a book we read, a delicious meal we cooked, and other random thoughts danced around in our heads. But if you had one or two people join you in prayer, there is a difference.

Action Steps

To practise corporate prayer, here are your action steps:

Identify at least two friends in the faith. Most times, it's better if they are in the same phase of life as you are; that is, students with students, the working class with the working class, and so on. This way, your schedules can easily mesh. Schedule a time for all of you to pray together and every day. It can be 15 minutes, it can be four hours, depending on your schedule. Do it consistently for 30 days. Write down instructions, victories, and testimonies that arise as a result.

CHAPTER FIVE

PRIVATE PRAYER TIME

x x x x x x x x

For all the blessings of corporate prayer, it can never and should never take the place of private prayers. There is a place in your devotions that has room for you and God only. Sometimes, corporate prayer can only go so far, especially where personal spiritual matters must be addressed. Two immediately become a crowd. Like in Gethsemane, you must leave Peter and John and move further to be alone with God.

Understand that private prayers share a symbiotic relationship with public prayers. In the sense that whilst it is true that public prayers help private prayers, it is equally true that private prayers help public prayers. When a person who has been with God leads a corporate prayer, the atmosphere immediately changes. You can tell that they seek to take people to a place they themselves have been. Enjoy public prayers all you want; the blessings are endless. But what happens after the program ends, people leave, chairs are stacked, and the venue is vacated? Now, you're left alone. What do you do then? Wait until the next service, which for most people happens only once a week?

This goes to show that limiting your prayer life to corporate prayer times alone will be disastrous. As a matter of fact, praying well corporately and having no private prayer life might be indicative of something more serious. The Lord Jesus describes as hypocrites the type of people who "pray to be seen." Harsh as it may seem, we must all test our motives in this regard. Let's learn from the words of Jesus in **Matthew 6:5:**

> *"And when thou prayest, thou shalt not be as the hypocrites are: for they love to pray standing in the synagogues and in the corners of the streets, that they may be seen of men. Verily I say unto you, They have their reward. But thou, when thou prayest, enter into thy closet, and when thou hast shut thy door, pray to thy Father which is in secret; and thy Father which seeth in secret shall reward thee openly."*

PRIVATE PRAYER TIME

Do not get this wrong. If you need help in your prayer life and exploit corporate prayer to get it done, there is absolutely nothing wrong with that. But you must beware of the tendency to feign a life of fervour when you are struggling in your private prayer life. Jesus describes such people as hypocrites. They love to pray quite alright, but it has to be in the open where they can be seen and commended. In fact, the praise and attention they get from the spectators is the only reward they get—nothing of eternal value. In reproving the religious leaders for their hypocritical public prayers, Jesus dropped a gem about private prayers. He said this:

> *"But thou, when thou prayest, enter into thy closet, and when thou hast shut thy door, pray to thy Father which is in secret; and thy Father which seeth in secret shall reward thee openly."*

What a promise! What an assurance! If I pray in secret, God will reward me openly. I don't need to show the world that I am prayerful. If I pray, I will have something to show. Private prayer will birth self-announcing testimonies in my life. Isn't that awesome?

I remember the first time I experienced this. I was to have a meeting with a fellow student leader in my undergraduate days.

As we met and walked to the meeting venue, she gave a gentle sigh to herself, and I discerned she literally exhaled glory. I was so astonished that I asked her immediately, "Have you been praying?" She said yes; she had just finished praying. Private prayer does more in us and for us than we realise.

If you want to fulfil God's plan for your life, you would have to cultivate a private prayer culture. Paul the Apostle gives you an assurance thus: "Meditate on these things; give yourself entirely to them, that your progress may be evident to all." **(1 Timothy 4:15)**. When you spend time with God, it will begin to show! It is, by the way, the privilege of your life that the almighty God wants you to build intimacy with Him. Take Him up on this offer!

Learning from Jesus

You think you know emotional pressure? Jesus did, too. In fact, He was so stressed, the Bible records that His sweat turned to droplets of blood. Some people think this was just a euphemism, but it's actually a medical condition known as hematohidrosis. Hematohidrosis (or hematidrosis) is a condition in which the blood vessels that feed the sweat glands rupture, causing them to ooze blood. This condition can occur under conditions of extreme physical or emotional stress.

PRIVATE PRAYER TIME

In that deep state of stress, Jesus talks to His Father and pours out His heart to the Lord. This is such a vital lesson, especially in the world we presently live in. When you feel overwhelmed, pray! It's okay that you cried. It is understandable that you feel overwhelmed. But the Lord Jesus models to us how to handle a life of pressure. The thought of Golgotha should drive you to Gethsemane. Pray and let strength rise from within you.

To the church at Philippi, Paul says: *"Be anxious for nothing, but in everything by prayer and supplication, with thanksgiving, let your requests be made known to God."* - **Philippians 4:6**

A lot of people stay away from prayer when they feel overwhelmed. That is such a counterproductive thing to do. You don't stay away from medication when you feel sick; rather you go seeking it. The same goes for emotional stress. You ought to gravitate towards the remedy. Build the discipline of a private prayer life. Not just to handle pressure in life, but to build intimacy with the Lord.

Jesus and His Private Prayer Life

The most humbling example of a private prayer life is that of the Lord Jesus Himself. If you thought for a moment that you could go through life without a vibrant private prayer life, the life of Jesus should make you think again. The incarnate Son of God showed us, by personal example, that we cannot and should not do life without prayer.

Looking through the four gospels, one obvious conclusion you will come to is that Jesus was a man of prayer. All four authors of the gospels had a lot to say about His prayer life. In fact, the words 'prayer' and 'pray' are used at least twenty-five times in connection with Jesus, and there are many instances in which the fact of His praying is mentioned where the words do not occur. Let's take a look at a couple of references:

- Mark, in his gospel, lets us know that Jesus was a person of morning prayer; He rose up very early to pray: **Mark 1:35** - *"Now in the morning, having risen a long while before daylight, He went out and departed to a solitary place; and there He prayed."*

    This goes to show that Jesus subscribed to the ancient tradition in most Christians homes of praying first thing in the morning. I believe that morning prayers are very essential. In this wicked world we live in, it is reckless to wake up, get dressed, and just step out of the house without praying first. Before you go into your day, like Jesus did, speak to the Lord in prayer and chart the course of your day.

- Not only did Jesus pray in the mornings, we also see that He prayed at night, sometimes, all through the night: **Luke 6:12** -

PRIVATE PRAYER TIME

"Now it came to pass in those days that He went out to the mountain to pray, and continued all night in prayer to God."

- It's also important to note that Jesus prayed following great feats. For example, after He fed five thousand people with five loaves and two fish, the Bible records: *"And when He had sent the multitudes away, He went up on the mountain by Himself to pray. Now when evening came, He was alone there."* - **Matthew 14:23**

After such a mighty feat, and with His fame spreading far and wide, you might expect that Jesus would take some time to bask in the thrill of all that was happening, or probably take some time off. However, we see that Jesus immediately went back to the place of prayer.

This goes to show that a private prayer life is not something you merely do as a form of preparation for a special event. Neither is it something you do only when there is a need. A private prayer life is an essential activity that must take place no matter what is happening. In the good times, you must pray; in the bad times, you must still pray. James, in his letter to the church, instructed acts of devotions as the response to both good and bad times. I like how he puts it: *"Is anyone among you suffering? Let him pray. Is anyone cheerful? Let him sing psalms."* **(James 5:15)**. This means that whether things are going well or not, you ought to talk to the Lord; be it with words or in songs.

Another important lesson from Jesus' private prayer life is that He was never too busy to pray. Luke records: *"However, the report went around concerning Him all the more; and great multitudes came together to hear, and to be healed by Him of their infirmities. So He Himself often withdrew into the wilderness and prayed."* **- Luke 5:15-16**

The more the fame of Jesus spread due to the mighty works He did, the more multitudes gathered for Him to minister to them. However, Jesus never—because of His hectic schedule—neglected the place of prayer. This is a mistake a lot of people make. They develop helpful and life-changing spiritual habits, and when the blessings come occasioned by those habits, they neglect the very habits that got them to where they are.

Be determined to maintain a life of private prayer. You must never be too busy for prayer. If you ever find yourself too busy to pray, then you are busier than God intends you to be. You must put structures in place to ensure you never relegate to the back seat what is important because of your schedule.

To the Wilderness

There is another vital thing to learn from Jesus here. The Bible says "He withdrew to the wilderness." Sometimes, you might have to leave the public eye; you might have to find your own "wilderness," somewhere people won't try to look for you. A quiet place where you can be alone with God for an extended period. It is called a "special season of devotions." Everyone needs this once in a while. If Jesus couldn't do without special seasons of devotions, you better not think that you can.

Do You See Your Need For God?

If you go one week or three days without praying, you are suggesting that you are self-sufficient. You believe you can live fine without God. It is most probably indicative of a heart that is not truly humbled before the Lord. That's the root cause of your struggle to keep a consistent private prayer life. No matter what you learn about prayer, if deep down, you think you can coast through life without God, you won't pray as often as you should. To you, prayer becomes like an addendum—useful but not necessary.

In the first sermon Jesus ever preached, He said: *"Blessed are the poor in spirit, for theirs is the kingdom of heaven."* **(Matthew 5:3)**. To be 'poor in spirit' is to be insufficient in yourself. To recognise that in and of yourself, you are spiritually bankrupt. You need God! This is the bedrock of a consistent prayer life. The realisation that you cannot do life on your own. This, by the way, is the posture of the heart that makes genuine conversion possible. Again, Jesus says about the poor in spirit, that "Theirs is the kingdom of heaven."

If we are as thoughtful as we ought to be, we would be much more prayerful. Every heart that belongs to Jesus ought not to believe he is self-sufficient. You must realise that you are all that you are because of God's grace, and wake up every day with an attitude of gratitude. This way, the floors in your room will always have a feel of your knees. You will frequently lie prostrate before God, and not just when you're in trouble. If you cultivate and continue in this attitude of gratitude, you will find it hard to go without praying.

A Simple Rule in Private Prayer

A lot of times, when it comes to spiritual devotions, we are carried away by the action, not necessarily the heart behind the action. As a result of this, we often miss God while looking for activities. We must never forget that God is Spirit. When the woman at the well quizzed Jesus if Jerusalem was the place to worship God, or the mountains where her ancestors worshipped, Jesus pointed her attention to a person, not to a location.

PRIVATE PRAYER TIME

John 4:24 says, "God is Spirit, and those who worship Him must worship in spirit and truth." So, because God is Spirit, the reason you do what you do matters more than the way you do it. You cannot deceive God with your activities; He can see your heart! Look at **1 Samuel 16:7**: *"But the Lord said to Samuel, 'Do not look at his appearance or at his physical stature, because I have refused him. For the Lord does not see as man sees; for man looks at the outward appearance, but **the Lord looks at the heart**.'"* (Emphasis added)

We have earlier emphasised the importance of prayer, especially having a private prayer life. However, you must realise that prayer is more than just a religious activity. When it comes to God, doing the right thing—albeit with the wrong intention—renders the entirety of your effort futile.

> *"When you pray, don't be like the hypocrites who love to pray publicly on street corners and in the synagogues where everyone can see them. I tell you the truth, that is all the reward they will ever get."*
> **- Matthew 6:5 NLT**

Jesus says here without mincing words that the reward for those who go about their devotions for the praises of men is the praises of men. This is so important. God judges the heart, not mere actions. Every time you pray, as your lips are speaking, your heart is also speaking. And the prayer that God is really particular about is what your heart is saying. You can be a professional when it comes to checking all the boxes of what prayer should look like. You know how to raise your voice and how to kneel, your prayer can even be so animated that observers are impressed. However, the best prayer posture before God is the posture of your heart. This is what makes your prayers powerful. The biggest instrument of prayer is not your voice or your gestures, but your heart!

> *"The Lord says: 'These people come near to me with their mouth and honour me with their lips, but their hearts are far from me. Their worship of me is based on merely human rules they have been taught.'"*
>
> **- Isaiah 29:13, NIV**

If you read a book on prayer and you don't learn this, you have not learnt prayer. Have you observed that when some people pray, they only go through the motions of giving God thanks because that is what traditionally precedes making requests? This is why many are often loud when we make requests and virtually inaudible when it's time to give thanks. Every time you give God thanks with your lips—not because you are truly grateful, but just so you can get to the part where you make requests, God sees it. This is why you must train yourself in the place of prayer to only utter words you mean.

Prayer is more than the words you utter when you pray. For example, when Hagar was stranded in the wilderness of Beersheba with the baby Ishmael, God answered Ishmael's cry:

> "But God heard the boy crying, and the angel of God called to Hagar from heaven, 'Hagar, what's wrong? Do not be afraid! God has heard the boy crying as he lies there. Go to him and comfort him, for I will make a great nation from his descendants.'"
> **– Genesis 21:17-18 NLT**

You would have thought that Hagar needed to purchase the bestselling prayer book of her time for God to hear her. However, God responded to the innocent cry of a child in distress. The same happened with the Israelites in Egypt, when they were under the tyranny of Pharaoh:

> *"Now it happened in the process of time that the king of Egypt died. Then the children of Israel groaned because of the bondage, and they cried out; and their cry came up to God because of the bondage. So God heard their groaning, and God remembered His covenant with Abraham, with Isaac, and with Jacob."*
>
> **- Exodus 2:23-24**

God's response didn't come off the back of a powerful 30-day prayer accompanied by dry fasting. God responded to the groans of the children of Israel due to the bondage they were under. This is not to talk down on seasons of fasting and prayer, but to make you see why fasting and prayer work. It is about your heart before God, not just the rigours of activity.

Eli could barely hear Hannah's words. Her speech was so unpolished, he assumed she was drunk. But God saw Hannah's heart. So, you see, prayer is not a game of eloquence. God is not checking how refined your speech is before He answers your petition. We learn also from the story of King Saul in **1 Samuel 13** that what God wanted was not a man who would make sacrifices, but a man after His own heart. This was the mistake that King Saul made. He thought sacrifice could make up for his disobedience:

PRIVATE PRAYER TIME

> *"And Samuel said to Saul, 'You have done foolishly. You have not kept the commandment of the Lord your God, which He commanded you. For now the Lord would have established your kingdom over Israel forever. But now your kingdom shall not continue. The Lord has sought for Himself a man after His own heart, and the Lord has commanded him to be commander over His people, because you have not kept what the Lord commanded you.'"*
>
> **- 1 Samuel 13:13-14**

King Saul was not after God's heart. This was again proven when He disobeyed God's instruction through the prophet Samuel to wipe out the Amalekites. King Saul instead preserved the life of the Amalekite king, and also offered the animals they took as spoils of war as sacrifices unto the Lord:

> "So Samuel said: 'Has the Lord as great delight in burnt offerings and sacrifices, as in obeying the voice of the Lord? Behold, to obey is better than sacrifice, and to heed than the fat of rams.'"
>
> **- 1 Samuel 15:22**

We can teach a lot of mechanical principles about prayer—talk about how to keep your prayer altar alive, use different techniques to get you to pray, and so on. But the state of your heart is a major issue. The sincerity of your heart is a leveller in the place of prayers. You may not have gone to a seminary, read as many books on prayer, or learnt many Greek words, but a broken and contrite heart will do mighty good for you in your prayer journey.

Tips on Cultivating a Private Prayer Life

- **Set an alarm:** Remember we talked earlier about the apostles having a time of prayer? It is important to have a prayer time and stick to it. It is so important that one can conclude that if you do not know when exactly you pray, you do not have a prayer life. Set a time and use your alarm clock as a reminder. As a rule, make sure you don't turn off the alarm without praying. At best, you can snooze, but never turn it off. Also, even if the time for prayer came and you were busy, pray for as much time as possible. Do not simply move on. Why? Because it takes that level of intentionality to build a new habit.

- **Use a countdown timer:** I used this hack at a time in my life when I felt down and didn't feel like praying. I'd set a countdown timer and wouldn't stop praying until I heard the timer go off. Even better, I'd set the countdown timer in tranches. So, if I was to pray for one hour, I would set the timer for twenty minutes and repeat it three times. This makes your prayer goal more achievable. Psychologically, you know you only have to go twenty minutes, and then another, and then another. It is funny how that makes more sense to your subconscious mind to break it down like this, but it works. You could also have a different prayer focus for each prayer segment.

- **Have a specific place:** Do you know the reason people struggle to work in their bedrooms because they might end up sleeping? It's not just that the bed is there. It is that your subconscious mind has registered the bedroom as a place for resting. Having a specific place you pray helps a lot. So, don't just have a prayer time, also have a prayer place.

- **Playlists:** Some people do not pray well with music playing, some others do. If your case is the latter, then having a playlist helps private prayer a great deal. Have playlists that cover the length of time you desire to pray. For instance, six songs of about five mins each will take you through one hour of prayer.

- **Create an atmosphere of prayer:** What you do when you are not praying can influence your prayer life. There are activities that, upon exposing yourself to constantly, you may not feel like praying. On the other hand, there are activities that encourage you to pray more. Learn to build an atmosphere of prayer as often as you can during the day, by listening to sermons and spirit-filled songs.

Action Steps

Your action steps for this chapter are quite simple. You are going to put to practise all the tips for a private prayer life that you just read at the end of this chapter.Set an Alarm

> *"Evening and morning and at noon I will pray, and cry aloud…"*
>
> **- Psalms 55:17a**

Build your schedule around a three-tiered prayer time. Set alarms to pray first thing in the morning, in the afternoon, and last thing at night. Ensure you stick to it. Use a countdown timer. Out of these three prayer times in a day, challenge yourself and ensure one of them is not less than an hour. To help you pray for long, divide the overall prayer time into smaller prayer segments. For

PRIVATE PRAYER TIME

the sake of this example, for one hour, split the hour in three parts of 20 minutes each, or four parts of 15 minutes each. You can change the focus of your prayer for each of the prayer segments. Do this consistently for 14 days. Complete the 14-day streak and start again. After every 14-day streak, increase the long prayer time by 30 minutes, if your schedule permits. Schedule a personal retreat. Set out a time for prayer and Bible study. It can be one day a week, or one week in a quarter. Set this time aside and stick to it.

CHAPTER SIX

HOW TO PRAY

(PRIORITIES IN PRAYER)

x x x x x x x x

One of the first things I learnt about prayer was perseverance. I was 12 years old when my father came to my room one morning. He tapped me and my sister, and said: "Get ready; we are praying all day today." As my sister and I began to prepare, I asked her, "Did he mean what he said?"

"He's joking," she answered.

But he was not. We started by 6:00 a.m. From then, the hours continued to roll by until we had prayed for 12 hours. Yes, you read right. 12 hours at age 12. I thought I was going to die, but I didn't. In fact, I sort of grew a chip on my shoulder after that event. I went around telling people about this accomplishment. "Have you prayed for 12 hours before? I have." Even when the conversation did not warrant it, I found a way to chip it in. I had to tell everyone, especially my friend's aunty. She was a pastor at a very vibrant, word-based ministry in this country. Whenever we visited, she would sit us in her living room and play sermons. Being kids, we hated it. We just wanted to watch movies. But after my 12-hour prayer feat, I now had something I could use to impress her.

So, on this particular visit, as was her custom, my aunt took me aside to teach me the gospel. I was literally champing at the bit, eager to share my news. So, when she asked, "How's your walk with God?," my answer leapt out of my mouth.

"Oh, very fine. In fact, recently, I prayed for 12 hours!"

My aunt's response to this shocked me. "Okay nice," she said, "But what did you pray?"

I had never heard such a question before. What do you mean, "*What* did I pray?" I prayed for 12 hours! You should be proud! But my aunt kept looking at me with concern written on her face. In my naivety, I thought she was jealous, maybe because she had never done such a thing in her life. What I didn't know at that time was that prayer is not just about how long you pray, or if you are praying at all. There is a "how" to prayer. As important as perseverance in prayer is, purpose is of more importance. You need to learn how to pray the right way.

It doesn't matter if you run a 100-metre race in four seconds. There are certain rules you must obey, or you will be disqualified. If you beat the gun, you wouldn't be given the prize. If you cross lanes, you wouldn't be given the prize. You must run circumspectly. Likewise, there are rules in the realm of the spirit. There is a way to pray. It's good to pray long, but it's more important to pray well.

Teach Us to Pray

> "Now it came to pass, as He was praying in a certain place, when He ceased, that one of His disciples said to Him, 'Lord, teach us to pray, as John also taught his disciples.'"
> **- Luke 11:1**

To reiterate the thought I shared at the introduction of this book, this text suggests that there is a better way to pray. The Jews are a very devout people. They were not strangers to devotions. Their forefathers were the patriarchs of faith; Abraham, Moses, David, and so on. But still, the very Jewish disciples of Jesus observed the prayer life of Jesus and asked Him to teach them to pray. They saw a better way.

Some of these guys were previously the disciples of John the Baptist. John had taught them to pray. The forerunner of the Messiah, who Jesus Himself acclaimed to be the greatest prophet **(Matthew 11:11)**, had taught the disciples to pray. This was a big deal. Yet, they observed the prayer life of Jesus and were fascinated enough to ask, "Teach us to pray." Friends, there is a better way to pray.

Secondly, just like the disciples of Jesus, it might surprise you to know that some people do not even know what to say when they pray. I have counselled people who even took out time to pray, got there and didn't know what to say. The common thing with them all is this question: "What do I pray about?"

For a lot of people, the challenge is that all they know about prayer is it being a medium to ask God for things. Hence, when there seems to be no material request to make to God, they find that they have nothing to say. Friends, to have a proper prayer life, you must look beyond your needs. Think about this: when Christ comes, He will wipe the tears from every eye, and there'd literally be no need to ask for. When we fellowship in heaven, what would you say, seeing as there won't be any needs?

While God is definitely not against us prospering materially, it cannot be the basis of our relationship with Him, or the only petition during our prayer times. If the only reason you pray is to ask God for things, when you have all you've been asking for, you will stop praying. Any philosophy you have concerning prayer that cannot sustain your prayer life after your requests have been granted is dangerous and not sustainable.

What Then Should Prayer Be About?

Let's draw lessons from what we call "The Lord's Prayer." There are awesome lessons on the priority of prayer.

1. **FELLOWSHIP WITH GOD**

    Since the entirety of the second chapter is on this, I won't spend time here. But it is noteworthy that Jesus said, "When you pray, say: Our Father in heaven." I know God is powerful and can meet your needs, but do you love God? Do you desire fellowship with Him? The context of your relationship with God should be His Fatherhood. That's the first priority in prayer.

2. **WORSHIP**

    Next, He says, "Hallowed be your name." In the place of prayer, we recognise God for who He is over our lives, and we respond appropriately with worship. One thing about prayer is that it helps you put God in His rightful place in your heart. Ever heard the saying, "You need to stop telling God about your problems and start telling your problems about God"? That is what prayer does to you. It magnifies the majesty of God in your consciousness. No true prayer session is ended without a renewed consciousness of God's hallowedness.

3. **CONSECRATION**

Jesus says to pray, "Your kingdom come, Your will be done on earth." This perspective to prayer seems to be foreign to many people. Whilst some only know to ask for what they want, the Bible teaches you to ask for what God wants. With prayer, you partner with the agenda of God. When you listen to the prayers of some Christians, you may begin to wonder, "Who exactly is the God in this relationship?" Because if it seems like God is the one constantly "serving you," then who really is the God in that relationship? Some have used Isaiah 45:11 as a scriptural basis for commanding God in prayer to do whatever they want. However, let's examine this verse of scripture together to know exactly what it says: *"Thus saith the LORD, the Holy One of Israel, and his Maker, Ask me of things to come concerning my sons, and concerning the work of my hands command ye me.'"* – **Isaiah 45:11 KJV**

On the surface, this might seem to imply that God is giving us the go ahead to command Him, but let's see what other translations say:

NET: *"This is what the Lord says, the Holy One of Israel, the one who formed him, concerning things to come: 'How dare you question me about my children! How dare you tell me what to do with the work of my own hands!'"*

NLT: *"This is what the Lord says—the Holy One of Israel and your Creator: 'Do you question what I do for my children? Do you give me orders about the work of my hands?'"*

How shocking is that? God was actually saying the opposite! He wasn't saying, "Go ahead and command me." Rather, He was rebuking those who did. God doesn't exist for our pleasure; we exist for His. He meets our needs because He loves us, but we live for Him. The priority of our prayer life must reflect that as well. In the place of prayer, we lay down our will to take upon God's. You will not fully explore the power of prayer if you do not understand this.

What Can I Pray About?

1. **SPIRITUAL GROWTH**

    My journey to understanding the priority of prayer was when I set out to study all the prayers in the New Testament about a decade ago. When I looked through them, I immediately saw that most prayers in the epistles were concerning spiritual growth. I saw that spiritual growth had to matter more to me than it did, and that if I was more mature spiritually, I won't even have some of the problems I had been praying about.

    Let's see some examples of scriptures on spiritual growth:

    a. **Ephesians 1:17-19** – "…that the God of our Lord Jesus Christ, the Father of glory, may give to you the spirit of wisdom and revelation in the knowledge of Him, the eyes of your understanding being enlightened; that you may know what is the hope of His calling, what are the riches of the glory of His inheritance in the saints, and what is the exceeding greatness of His power toward us who believe, according to the working of His mighty power."

    Here, Paul's prayer is that you will receive spiritual insight into all that Christ has done for you. He desires that you will know the "hope of his calling"—the reason

Jesus came to the world; and "the riches of the glory of His inheritance in the saints —the lavish nature of the benefits of salvation that you have received."

b. **Ephesians 3:16-19** – "...that He would grant you, according to the riches of His glory, to be strengthened with might through His Spirit in the inner man, that Christ may dwell in your hearts through faith; that you, being rooted and grounded in love, may be able to comprehend with all the saints what is the width and length and depth and height— to know the love of Christ which passes knowledge; that you may be filled with all the fullness of God."

Here, Paul prays for strength that can only come by the Spirit of God inside you. Then he prays that you will fully understand the extent of God's love for you. This is such a powerful prayer to pray very often.

c. **Philippians 1:9-11** – "And this I pray, that your love may abound still more and more in knowledge and all discernment, that you may approve the things that are excellent, that you may be sincere and without offence till the day of Christ, being filled with the fruits of righteousness which are by Jesus Christ, to the glory and praise of God."

Here, Paul is praying that you grow in your love walk and in the expressions of the fruits that accompany the nature of righteousness which you now have in Christ.

d. **Colossians 1:9-10** – "For this reason we also, since the day we heard it, do not cease to pray for you, and to ask that you may be filled with the knowledge of His will in all wisdom and spiritual understanding; that you may walk worthy of the Lord, fully pleasing Him, being fruitful in every good work and increasing in the knowledge of God."

Paul's prayer here is centred on you knowing God's will for your life, and living a life that pleases Him. This is such a powerful prayer of consecration. Other powerful prayers on consecration include:

e. **2 Thessalonians 1:11-12** – "Therefore we also pray always for you that our God would count you worthy of this calling, and fulfil all the good pleasure of His goodness and the work of faith with power, that the name of our Lord Jesus Christ may be glorified in you, and you in Him, according to the grace of our God and the Lord Jesus Christ."

f. Hebrews 13:20-21 – "Now may the God of peace who brought up our Lord Jesus from the dead, that great Shepherd of the sheep, through the blood of the everlasting covenant, make you complete in every good work to do His will, working in you what is well pleasing in His sight, through Jesus Christ, to whom be glory forever and ever. Amen."

1. PRAY FOR PEOPLE

Anyone who doesn't know what to pray, doesn't pray for people. When you pray for people, there will always be too much to pray about. The Bible instructs us to bear one another's burdens **(Galatians 6:2)**. This is why, as the Church, we all need one another. Paul, in his epistle to Corinth, says, *"And the eye cannot say to the hand, 'I have no need of you,' nor again the head to the feet, 'I have no need of you.'"* **(1 Corinthians 12:21)**. Your prayers aren't meant to be about you alone; you have a responsibility to pray for others. Here is a list of prayer points for other people:

HOW TO PRAY

- **The unsaved**

"For this is good and acceptable in the sight of God our Saviour, who desires all men to be saved and to come to the knowledge of the truth."

–1 Timothy 2:3-4

To be clear, prayer cannot take the place of evangelism. You must preach to the lost. However, praying for them will also go a long way. That the scales of the deceiver will fall off their eyes, so they can discern the truth **(2 Corinthians 4:3-5)**. If you have loved ones who are yet unsaved, you have a lot to pray about! The salvation of the unsaved is the number one heartbeat of God.

- **Ministry gifts and missionaries**

Just like in the case of Peter in Acts 12, praying for ministers of the gospel can be the difference between life and death. In one of the shortest verses in the entire Bible, you can feel the weight of Paul's words when he says: *"Brethren, pray for us."* (1 Thessalonians 5:25)

So, what do you pray? Here are a few scriptures:

"Finally, brethren, pray for us, that the word of the Lord may run swiftly and be glorified, just as it is with you."
- 2 Thessalonians 3:1

"And for me, that utterance may be given to me, that I may open my mouth boldly to make known the mystery of the gospel, for which I am an ambassador in chains; that in it I may speak boldly, as I ought to speak."
- Ephesians 6:19-20

"Meanwhile praying also for us, that God would open to us a door for the word, to speak the mystery of Christ, for which I am also in chains, that I may make it manifest, as I ought to speak."
Colossians 4:3-4 -

- **Persecuted Christians around the world**
  This is one prayer deficiency in the Church. It is my personal opinion that we do not uphold the persecuted

in prayer enough. The Bible is specific about how invested we ought to be in the plights of other believers. It says: *"Remember the prisoners as if chained with them—those who are mistreated—since you yourselves are in the body also."* **(Hebrews 13:3)** Here are a few things you can pray about:

Pray for them to be comforted. 2 Corinthians 1:3-4 - "Blessed be the God and Father of our Lord Jesus Christ, the Father of mercies and God of all comfort, who comforts us in all our tribulation, that we may be able to comfort those who are in any trouble, with the comfort with which we ourselves are comforted by God."

Pray for their deliverance. 2 Thessalonians 3:2 – "And that we may be delivered from unreasonable and wicked men; for not all have faith."

"Yes, we had the sentence of death in ourselves, that we should not trust in ourselves but in God who raises the dead, who delivered us from so great a death, and does deliver us; in whom we trust that He will still deliver us."

- 2 Corinthians 1:9-10

"He shall call upon Me, and I will answer him; I will be with him in trouble; I will deliver him and honour him."

- Psalms 91:15

- **The Body of Christ and other Christians..**
We also have a responsibility to intercede for our local assemblies and the Body of Christ in general. It is important to note that Paul's prayers concerning spiritual growth were for the entire Church.

Prayer points for the Body of Christ:

That the Body stands strong in the face of opposition.

That our convictions are preserved. That our message is amplified around the world, by the Spirit.at signs accompany our message as we preach.

- **Family and friends.**
Prayer points: That they know the Lord and grow in Him.That they are kept from all evil. That their needs are met.

- **Your nation and those in power.**
Prayer points: That peace reigns (Psalms 122:7)That the

gospel prospers in your nation. That the righteous are in power.

2. **PRAYER FOR OUR NEEDS**

While I have emphasised that the primary purpose of prayer is not for God to meet your needs, you must know that God is interested in your needs being met. He wants you to prosper and be in health, even as your soul prospers **(3 John 1:2)**. If God could give us His highest treasure in His son, He can give us all other things as well. Cast every care before the Lord in prayer.

Action Steps

Here is a list of prayer points for your private prayer time:

SPIRITUAL GROWTH

Father, flood the eyes of my understanding with the light of your truth. I know and understand your provision of salvation in Jesus, and all that accrues to me as a result of His sacrifice. I grow increasingly conscious of the power at work in me. I grow increasingly conscious of the presence of God in me. It must show in signs and wonders that my eyes have seen the glory of the Lord. Today, I receive the strength only the Spirit gives. In my mind, my body, and in my spirit; I am strengthened. I declare that I am constantly aware of the extent of God's love for me. I am the beloved of God. This is my life. And this I pray, that God's love may abound in my heart, and that I may grow and more in knowledge and in all discernment; that I may approve the things that are excellent, that I may be sincere and without offence until the day of Christ; being filled with the fruits of righteousness which are by Jesus Christ, to the glory and praise of God. Righteousness is my nature in Christ, and it is evident. My life is a testimony of the fruits of righteousness. It shows in my conduct, in my speech, in my thoughts, and in my actions. I am full of the love of God. I declare that I am continually at the centre of God's will for my life. I know God's will and I do it. I live a life worthy of the calling.

PRAYERS FOR MINISTRY GIFTS AND MISSIONARIES

Father, as I speak to (insert the name of the person to whom you are currently sharing the good news), let your Spirit convict them of your truth. Let them experience your love and believe in your salvation. I declare that a door of utterance is open to men of God and missionaries in cities that have hitherto shut their doors to the message of the gospel. The good news of Jesus prevails in these cities until the knowledge of God covers the earth. I pray that through the work of every sincere ministry, the word of God prospers mightily and spreads rapidly.

HOW TO PRAY

PRAYERS FOR PERSECUTED CHRISTIANS

I pray that every Christian going through persecution experiences the comfort that the Spirit gives. Their minds are fortified with the peace of God, and their faith remains resilient in adversity by the power of the Spirit of God. I decree supernatural intervention for every Christian facing persecution. By the power of God, ways are made in the desert, paths are open in the forest, and light shines in darkness.

PRAYERS FOR THE BODY OF CHRIST AND OTHER CHRISTIANS

The Church of God in this country prevails over adversity. We are constantly in the will of God, and our testimony is preserved across generations. I declare that a mighty display of signs and wonders accompanies the preaching of the gospel in my day. We see the manifestation of compelling power that transforms lives and delivers the oppressed.

PRAYERS FOR FAMILY AND FRIENDS

I decree that everyone connected to me grows strong in the Lord. They are full of the Spirit and their faith fails not. I declare that everyone connected to me is protected. We are not casualties of these last days. When evil is passing through the land, we are clearly marked and safe in Goshen.

PRAYERS FOR YOUR NATION

I insist relentlessly that peace and prosperity reigns in my country. Righteous leadership is exalted, and cruelty in leadership is judged swiftly. I decree that in this nation, the gospel of Jesus prevails. People who will tear down satanic architecture and institute kingdom systems are raised into power. Jesus reigns supreme.

CHAPTER SEVEN

HOW NOT TO PRAY

xxxxxxxx

One of the best ways to understand what something is, is to know what it isn't. You truly know a thing when you can differentiate it from other things. Almost as much as the Lord Jesus teaches us how to pray, He also teaches us how *not* to pray.

1. **Praying to be seen**: There is something about long prayers that tends to puff up the ego of some. You might want to watch out for that. Do you really need to announce how long you prayed? I know it seems common, but is it necessary? I talked about this in earlier chapters, but let me remind you again. Jesus said, *"And when you pray, you shall not be like the hypocrites. For they love to pray standing in the synagogues and on the*

corners of the streets, that they may be seen by men. Assuredly, I say to you, they have their reward." **(Matthew 6:5)**.

Isn't it scary that Jesus said if you pray to be seen, you have your reward? If you are wondering what this reward is, it is that you are applauded by men. Such people have no reward in prayers aside from that, and they shouldn't expect such prayers to be answered.

2. **Don't use vain repetitions**: Another way Jesus taught us not to pray is the use of vain repetitions. Jesus says, *"But when ye pray, use not vain repetitions, as the heathen do: for they think that they shall be heard for their much speaking. Be not ye therefore like unto them: for your Father knoweth what things ye have need of, before ye ask him."* **(Matthew 6:7-8)**

This particular text appears to be quite confusing for a number of Christians. This is because when Jesus was going to teach on prayer in Luke 11, He emphasised what is known as importunity in prayer. Importunity refers to persistence in prayer. However, persistence will involve some form of repetition. This then begs the question, was Jesus contradicting Himself?

Importunity in prayer is a very vital principle in prayer; in fact, Jesus practised it. At the Garden of Gethsemane, Jesus had just one prayer point: *"Father, let this cup pass over me."* He prayed the same prayer for about three hours. Point is, not all repetition is vain. In **Revelation 4:8**, the Bible records, "The four living creatures, each having six wings, were full of eyes around and within. And they do not rest day or night, saying: 'Holy, holy, holy, Lord God Almighty, Who was and is and is to come!'"

These heavenly creatures, for all of eternity, have been repeating the same words, yet it is not vain because they are doing it in worship—not for God to hear them because of the multitude of their words. What exactly is the difference between importunity in prayer and vain repetitions? The short answer is this: **MOTIVE!**

Let's examine Jesus' words again. He said "But when ye pray, use not vain repetitions, as the heathen do: for they think that they shall be heard for their much speaking."

Can you see that the problem wasn't that they prayed the same prayer or used the same words, but their motive. The practitioners of vain repetition seemed to have some religious formulas for the number of words they needed to use. Respectfully, there are some religious sects that have fixed words that must be routinely recited. Jesus abominates any form of prayer that focuses on the routine and the number of words spoken.

Cast your mind to Elijah taunting the Prophets of Baal. He asked them to pray louder so their god could hear them. Guess what? They did! They even went as far as cutting themselves. The idea that except you put up religious theatrics, God won't hear you is unchristian. God answers prayers because he is a loving God; not because we exert ourselves or say the right words, the right amount of times. For instance, repetitively reciting prayers of consecration is not vain repetition. You're not repeating so God can hear. You're repeating so the flesh can go under. Likewise, repeatedly affirming God's word over yourself is not vain repetition. Rather, you are doing it for your mind to be conscious of what God has said about you.

In conclusion, believe that God hears you when you pray, and persist in prayer. However, do not think that God hears you because of the multitude of your words. That is vain repetition.

3. **Praying to consume it upon your lusts**: This buttresses what we discussed in the chapter on the priority of prayer. The Bible says: "You ask and do not receive, because you ask

amiss, that you may spend *it* on your pleasures." **(James 4:3 KJV)**. There is such a thing as asking amiss. People who have no consecration or fellowship but are constantly bombarding God with requests fall into this category. God is not a genie, and He doesn't exist for our pleasure; we exist for His.

4. **Praying in strife:** Here is a scripture a lot of people do not seem to know: **1 Peter 3:7** – "Husbands, likewise, dwell with *them* with understanding, giving honour to the wife, as to the weaker vessel, and as *being* heirs together of the grace of life, that your prayers may not be hindered."

Yes, you read right. Strife can hinder your prayers! This is why Jesus says in **Matthew 5:23-24**, "Therefore if you bring your gift to the altar, and there remember that your brother has something against you, leave your gift there before the altar, and go your way. First be reconciled to your brother, and then come and offer your gift."

Devotions and strife do not go hand in hand. A lot of Christians are comfortable beefing half the nation and even family members whilst praying to God every day. It simply does not work that way. Perhaps you never read the terms and conditions as stated in The Lord's Prayer: "And forgive us our debts, as we forgive our debtors." **(Matthew 6:12)**

If you are not ready to forgive, you might as well close this book. Learning about prayer won't do you much good. I know it may be hard for you to forgive, but God is not asking you to forgive anyone because they deserve it, but because He forgave you. Please do not let anything hinder your prayers. No situation deserves that much power over your future.

Action Steps

For this chapter, you are going to pray three important prayers: Father, I repent of unforgivingness. I let go of everyone I have held in my heart. I forgive anyone who has wronged me, just as you have freely forgiven me. Father, you are Lord of my life, anything that competes for your place in my heart, I lay them on the altar of prayer today and I set them ablaze. Father, I submit my heart to you. Purge it of selfish desires and ambitions. I seek you and you alone.

CHAPTER EIGHT

FERVENCY IN PRAYER

×××××××

A couple of years back, while interacting with a particular lady, I asked her why she attended the church she was in then. It was a particular orthodox denomination at the time. She said the reason was her temperament. She liked things being quiet and solemn; hence, she only attended churches with solemn services. She felt charismatic people, for instance, were too ecstatic; and they shout too much in their services.

I thought that was interesting because this lady probably wouldn't have loved the way Jesus went about his devotions. The Bible records, "On the last day, that great day of the feast, Jesus stood and cried out, saying, 'If anyone thirsts, let him come to Me and drink!'" **(John 7:37)**.

I believe that Jesus preached like a charismatic preacher. When He spoke, you could tell how much passion He had for the words He spoke. This was so evident that after one of Jesus' sermons, the Bible records, "And so it was, when Jesus had ended these sayings, that the people were astonished at His teaching, for He taught them as one having authority, and not as the scribes." **(Matthew 7:28-29)**. He must have preached with so much gusto!

Now you must also realise that Jesus' passion and fervour wasn't only discernible in His preaching; we also see the same in His prayer life. At Gethsemane, the Bible records that "He went a little farther and fell on His face, and prayed, saying, 'O My Father, if it is possible, let this cup pass from Me; nevertheless, not as I will, but as You will.'" **(Matthew 26:39)**. Jesus fell on his face! He wasn't just casual about the prayer; He wasn't just reciting words to fulfil a prayer quota. You could see how much it meant to Him.

Another good observation here is that despite the fact that Jesus went further away from where the disciples were, what He said was heard. This means that Jesus must have prayed out loud. When Jesus fell on his face, He prayed with passion. No wonder the writer of the book of Hebrews had this to say about the prayer life of Jesus: "During the days of Jesus' life on earth, He offered up prayers and petitions with fervent cries and tears to the one who could save Him from death, and He was heard because of His reverent submission." **(Hebrews 5:7 NIV)**

Jesus prayed fervent prayers! This goes to show that your demeanour when it comes to prayer should not be subject to your temperament or your personality. Jesus is our perfect example. When we observe the prayer life of Jesus, we see that prayer must be fervent!

The interesting thing about people who use their temperament as an excuse for being cold in the place of prayer is that when their favourite football team scores a goal, for example, their temperament will not matter at that point; their rejoicing and jubilation will be as hysterical as that of every other person in the room. I will even go as far as saying that your temperament goes out of the way when it comes to something you truly care about. Have you ever considered that the reason you are not as fervent as you should be in the place of prayer isn't because you are not someone who shouts, but it is probably because you are yet to be emotionally consumed by what you are praying about.

Let's take another look at Jesus. The Bible lets us know that as He prayed at Gethsemane, his sweats were like droplets of blood. I explained earlier what this phenomenon is scientifically, and that it can happen under conditions of extreme physical or emotional stress. You can only imagine how consumed Jesus was by that prayer. While I'm not saying that until your sweat droplets become blood, you are yet to pray, it still highlights the importance of discernable fervour in the place of prayer. Are you truly consumed by what you are praying about? If you are, it will show in your tone and body posture. Like Jesus, there are times when you will have to pray with "loud cries."

It is unlikely that a prayer that cannot change your posture will change your life. I'm not making a doctrine out of this. I'm simply saying that care and sincerity are important in prayer—if you care, it will show.

Another example we see in the scriptures is Hannah at Shiloh in **1 Samuel 1:9-16**. The Bible records that even though Eli couldn't hear her words, Hannah's countenance and body language revealed someone who was totally consumed by what she was praying about.

Heartfelt Prayer

Concerning prayer, the apostle James writes: "The effectual fervent prayer of a righteous man availeth much." **(James 5: 16b, KJV)**. The word 'availeth' used in that scripture above is the Greek/Hebrew word *ischuō* which means "to prevail." This is the same word used in **Acts 19: 20**: "So mightily grew the word of God and *prevailed*." It means to wax strong/be of strength. The scripture above emphasises the fact that for the prayer of a righteous man to prevail, it has to be effectual and fervent.

It might interest you to know that the phrase 'effectual fervent' in Greek is one word *energeo*. It is the word from which we get the English word *energetic*, and it refers to a kind of energy that in itself will produce results. What is fervour? According to the Oxford English Dictionary, fervour means to have very strong feelings or enthusiasm about something. Other synonyms include intense feelings, passion, zeal, and ardour.

From the definition above, fervour in prayer means enthusiastic, passionate, zealous, intense prayer! Think about it. How was Jesus praying before His disciples asked Him to teach them to pray? When you are fervent in your prayer, even those watching can tell. Fervent prayer never hides. One thing that is obvious from the definition of fervent prayer is that it has to involve your emotions. Prayer is not just a religious exercise. It is a proof-producing venture. Earlier, I made mention of people in scripture who prayed fervent prayers. The first example was Jesus, our perfect example:

> *"He prayed more fervently, and he was in such agony of spirit that his sweat fell to the ground like great drops of blood."*
> **(Luke 22: 44, NLT)**

Imagine how passionate the prayer must have been for Jesus to have presented like that. Now, you must note that Jesus wasn't the only example of fervent prayer in the Bible. We can say Jesus is the saviour and was facing death, hence He had to pray like that. However, it was recorded in the Bible that "ordinary people" like you and me prayed just as fervently. One such person is Elijah. Below are four marks of discernible fervour:

1. **Posture**: Most times, when we talk about posture in prayer, people think it is only the posture of the heart that is being referred to. While that is important, it is not all. This mark of fervour speaks to both the heart and the physical posture we take while praying. The posture of the heart to take is that of sincerity and truth. Jeremiah says: "

FERVENCY IN PRAYER

When our prayer is sincere and our emotions are all in, our body tends to follow suit. It's not rocket science. When your heart is involved in something, your body and actions naturally gravitate towards that thing. If your heart's in it, your body will follow suit.

Jesus prayed and He fell to his face—that's a posture of fervent prayer! **(Matthew 26: 39)** We have established that Elijah prayed fervently, but let's buttress this point even more by showing examples of how Elijah's posture changed while he was praying. Elijah told King Ahab that he could hear the sound of an abundance of rain, but Elijah didn't stop there. While King Ahab ate, Elijah bent down to the ground and put his face between his knees **(1 Kings 18: 42)**.

This is why you are encouraged to sit up, stand up, or walk around when you want to pray. If you remain in bed, the chances that you will pray fervently are slimmer because you are still in your comfort zone. Have you ever seen someone who just received gripping news? You would rarely see such a person lying still in bed. Rather, their physical posture will reveal their state of heart. The person would most likely be visibly frantic. It must be the same in prayer. When you are consumed by the prayer, you might pace the floor, kneel, roll, lift your hands, or do whatever action that expresses how you feel.

2. **Tone:** Just like with posture, if your emotions are invested in something, it will show in the tone of your voice. This point is obvious when you watch people argue. They could start in a normal tone, but the moment the argument gets heated and their emotions get even more invested, they begin to inflect and raise their voices. This is why one discernible mark of fervent prayer is tone. For those of you who have prayed fervently, you know what it means to pray so fervently that you return home with a cracked voice and you won't even be bothered about it, because a broken voice is definitely better than a broken life.

3. **Concentration:** Concentration is simply focusing on just one thing for a set period of time. It sounds easy, right? But it's easier said than done, especially in this age and time. Concentration today is a rarity because things like social media and streaming sites have given us the option to go through thousands of opinions, ideas, and films, in such a short time that we now think concentrating on one thing is taboo. However, to pray fervently, one has to focus on a prayer point and stay there.

To practise and perfect concentration in prayer, we have to start by separating ourselves; first from our devices, and ultimately from people, just like Jesus did. He separated

FERVENCY IN PRAYER

Himself when it was time to pray and this is something we ought to emulate. It may not be easy and will demand a lot from us, but we need to be disciplined enough to work on ourselves. The truth is, if you get your concentration right, the rest will flow.

Have you noticed that when the generator goes off after being on for some hours, you can still hear the sound of the generator in your subconscious, even if you cover your ears? That's exactly what happens when you fill your mind with social media information, movies, football and the like. When you close your eyes to pray, that is exactly what will be replaying. This is why it is important to build a culture of stillness if you want to get to the point where you can pray as fervently as Jesus and Elijah. When it is time for prayer, set aside every form of distraction. You can go to a secluded place to be free from external distractions. If your phone will take your attention away, put it aside. Do everything to ensure that your prayer time truly counts.

4. **Consistency:** A lot of times, we hear quotes about successful people not exactly being the natural bests, but being the most consistent. This is true in every aspect of life, including our prayer life. To be more fervent in prayer, you need consistency. Consistency is what brings all the other marks of

fervency in prayer together. Without consistency, you can't learn to concentrate during prayer because it is not a day's job. Without consistency, you can't get to the point where your emotions are sold out to the prayer that your posture and tone change.

There's a popular phrase that people use, which has some element of truth, but can be somewhat misleading. When people say, "You learn how to pray by praying," what it actually means is that no matter how proficient you are, when it comes to the doctrine of prayer, you will only build or develop a prayer life by exercising yourself in prayer consistently. Every good thing indeed takes time, and fervency in prayer is not exempted. We need to grow in our staying power. We need to be able to pray about one thing for a very long time and not relent. Some people tend to stop praying when the time is up, but sometimes, the mark of fervency in prayer is not stopping until you see the answer to the prayer; just like Elijah when he was waiting for the rain to fall. He went back to pray seven different times **(1 Kings 18: 42-45)**.

Now, this doesn't mean that taking breaks between prayers isn't a mark of consistency. It is. As long as, like Jesus, when you take a break, you return to the place of prayer and continue with that same fervour, you are still being consistent **(Matthew 26: 40-42)**. Sometimes, it is difficult for us to involve our emotions in prayer, but the truth is, if our emotions are not involved, that isn't prayer, because prayer has more to do with our hearts than with our words. That means a prayer full of groanings and tears can speak better than a prayer of 10,000 mindless words being muttered. Above are clear marks to discern fervour in prayer. If any of those marks are lacking in your prayer, it is time to adjust.

Why Fervent Prayer?

In case it wasn't clear before, this is why you should aspire to fervent prayer:

1. **Fervent prayer gets the job done.** You should pray fervently because it is written in the Bible that fervent prayer avails much **(James 5:16b)**. There is so much that the Bible has said about believers and all that we are supposed to be walking in, but if you are too cool, calm, and collected, you may never touch the promises of God. Elijah already heard the sound of mighty rain coming but he still had to pray before even the first drop touched the ground. Hannah was seen praying fervently in the temple and her request came to pass **(1 Samuel 1:9-17)**. It has been proven that every time fervent prayer is made, it gets the job done.

2. **Fervent prayer creates a ripple amongst believers.** Everything Jesus did was marked by fervour. Because of how fervent Jesus was, His disciples recalled what was written in **Psalms 69:9**—"...the zeal of your house will consume me." **(John 2:13-17)**. Jesus' fervour in all things, including prayer, was so discernible that it was clear for all to see, and the people testified. Jesus was not cold, sluggish, or lazy towards the things of God. This is what the disciples and all those who followed Him saw and wanted to emulate. This is the reason that His disciples asked Him to teach them to pray. They liked what He was doing and wanted the same for themselves. As believers, we belong to a family of people who are at different levels spiritually. It is a good thing for another believer to see how fervently you pray and want to emulate that. What that does is, it creates a ripple in which when that person covets the grace upon your life and acquires it, somebody else can see that same thing in that person's life and want it, too. In other words, your fervency should be worth emulating. People should be able to covet your prayer life.

Action Steps

In this chapter, you learnt the four marks of discernible fervour. Your exercise here will be to put them to practise in a short time of prayer.

FERVENCY IN PRAYER

1. For the next 15 minutes, pray this:

   As I pray now, power is made available. I stir up the wonder-working power of God from my inside to change situations around me. As I pray now, everything the power of God can accomplish in my life is made possible.

   As you pray this prayer, ensure you consciously practise the four marks of fervour.

   a. **Posture** - Take a prayer posture. Prayer is serious business. It must show in your posture. Stand, kneel, bend. Take a posture that conveys the seriousness of what you are about to do.

   b. **Tone** - Pray loud for the entire duration of the 15 minutes.

   c. **Concentration** - Ensure you have no distractions. Put your phone away. You can even put all your electronic gadgets in one room and pray in another. If you find your mind wandering, pray in your understanding by repeating the words of the prayer point.

   d. **Consistency** - Ensure you practise these marks every time you pray.

CHAPTER NINE
RUNAWAY KNOCKS

×××××××

Did you ever have a mischievous neighbour who would knock on your door and run away? Or perhaps you were that mischievous neighbour? Imagine how puzzled anyone would have been to hear a knock on the door, open it, and find no one waiting outside. Sadly, this is the picture of our prayer lives sometimes. In fact, the exact metaphor of knocking on a door was used by the Lord Jesus to teach us prayer: *"Ask, and it will be given to you; seek, and you will find; knock, and it will be opened to you."* - **Matthew 7:7**

The phrases used here actually signify that we are to seek (or pray) with earnestness, diligence, and perseverance. In fact, the New Living Translation puts it this way: "Keep on asking, and you will receive what you ask for. Keep on seeking, and you will find. Keep on knocking, and the door will be opened to you." Sometimes, we are not just patient enough when we knock. We lose patience and we leave before the door is opened. Which is why one of the first and most important lessons we must learn about prayer is perseverance. This chapter is one of the most important chapters in this book. The thought in this chapter can be summarised in this simple quote: "If you have not learnt to persevere, you have not learnt to pray."

The amplified version of **James 5:16b** reads: "The earnest (heartfelt, continued) prayer of a righteous man makes tremendous power available [dynamic in its working]." Listen, there is a type of prayer that makes power available. That prayer is heartfelt. That prayer is continued. If your prayer will make tremendous power available, you are going to have to learn to persevere. You are going to have to learn to stay with God.

How Perseverance in Prayer Saved Peter's Life

I believe one of the best stories to teach the importance of perseverance in the place of prayer is Peter's supernatural deliverance from prison and death. Let's look at **Acts 12:1-5**:

PRAYBOOK

> *"Now about that time Herod the king stretched forth his hands to vex certain of the church. And he killed James, the brother of John, with the sword. And because he saw it pleased the Jews, he proceeded further to take Peter also. (Then were the days of unleavened bread.) And when he had apprehended him, he put him in prison, and delivered him to four quaternions of soldiers to keep him; intending after Easter to bring him forth to the people. Peter therefore was kept in prison: but prayer was made without ceasing of the church unto God for him."*

It was persecution. Herod rose against the church, seized James, and killed him. The Church looked on while this happened. They must have been in despair. But their troubles were not over. Herod struck again. He took Peter. This time the Church got angry! The writer of Acts says prayer was made *without ceasing* for Peter. They knew that they could not watch as Peter was also taken and killed. So, they stayed in the place of prayer. They must have prayed for days. Necessity demanded that they prayed until something happened.

Friend, something *did* happen. The Bible says that when Herod was about to bring Peter out to be killed, that night Peter was sleeping bound with two chains between two soldiers. That was not all the security. There were guards at the door of the prison also. But, you see, the Church was praying. What is a locked door? What are chains? Who are guards? That night, as a result of the persistent prayers of the Church, an angel appeared in Peter's prison cell, and the chains that bound Peter fell off. That night, the angel walked Peter past the two soldiers, past the guards, and into the street. That same night, Peter knocked on the door of the house where the Church was gathered, and met them praying. The Church had prayed until their answer literally came knocking on their door. Perseverance in prayer saved Peter's life. You must know that there are certain situations you will face, your only option would be to pray until something changes.

Psalms 115:16 says, *"The heaven, even the heavens, are the Lord's; but the earth He has given to the children of men."* When God created mankind, he gave us dominion over the earth. When Adam fell, he ceded that authority to Satan. As a result, things will happen on earth that are not in accordance with the will of God, but are a direct result of the whims of men or the manipulation of the enemy. Case in point, James' and Peter's arrest by Herod.

You must realise that prayer is the means through which we enforce the will of God in our situation. Prayer is the part a believer must play to secure God's intervention in a matter. There are matters you must sit on. Persevering in the place of prayer displays absolute trust in God. The Church prayed for Peter without ceasing because they believed there was something their prayers could do.

Dear believer, your response to hardship is not to sit and mope in despair. Neither is it to question God. Don't respond to trouble like a carnal man. Pray! Pray about that challenge. Stay in the place of prayer.

Why Pray Long?

What does it mean to persevere? It means to maintain a purpose in spite of difficulty or discouragement. There are many excuses not to pray for long hours; tiredness, laziness, or a busy schedule. However, in spite of this, you must learn to persevere in the place of prayer.

1. **WE PRAY LONG SO WE DO NOT FALL INTO TEMPTATION.**

    When Jesus faced Golgotha, He went along with His disciples to pray. He knew a trying time was ahead, both for Him and His disciples. He also knew prayer was the only way to build strength. To face Golgotha, Gethsemane was necessary. However, it was not yet one hour when Jesus came to find His disciples sleeping. Matthew 26:40 tells us: "And he cometh unto the disciples, and findeth them asleep, and saith unto Peter, 'What, could ye not watch with me one hour?'" Then Jesus said to them, "Watch and pray, that ye enter not into temptation: the spirit indeed is willing, but the flesh is weak." **(Matthew 26:41)**

Earlier, Jesus had told them, "Tarry ye here and watch with me." The word rendered "watch" means, literally, to abstain from sleep; then to be vigilant, or to guard against danger. This word is the same word rendered "vigilant" in **1 Peter 5:8** – "Be sober, be vigilant; because your adversary the devil walks about like a roaring lion, seeking whom he may devour."

Dear friend, STAY AWAKE! BE VIGILANT! Why? You have an adversary! The devil is after you. He seeks to have you and sift you as wheat until only the chaff remains. He seeks to trip you up with temptations. Your only security is to watch and pray always! Like the words of an old hymn say:

Christian seek not yet repose
Hear thy guardia angel say
Thou art in the midst of foes
Watch and pray

Watch and pray. A Christian who does not pray will be a Christian with contradictions.

2. **WE PRAY LONG SO WE CAN PRAY SHORT.**

In 1 Kings 17:1, Elijah declares that there will not be rain in Israel: "And Elijah the Tishbite, of the inhabitants of Gilead, said to Ahab, 'As the Lord God of Israel lives, before whom I stand, there shall not be dew nor rain these years, except at my word.'" For a space of three years, it was just as Elijah said—there was no rain. But you see, something happened behind the scenes that was not recorded in the book of 1 Kings. James, however, gives us a clearer picture:

"Elijah was a man with a nature like ours [with the same physical, mental, and spiritual limitations and shortcomings], and he prayed intensely for it not to rain, and it did not rain on the earth for three years and six months. Then he prayed again, and the sky gave rain and the land produced its crops [as usual]."
- James 5:17-18 (AMP)

At first read, you may be tempted to think that Elijah made a declaration and rain ceased. But with more information from James, we see that Elijah prayed intensely before making that proclamation. In 1 Kings chapter 18, Elijah then makes the declaration that rain will return. Here we see the action that backed that proclamation. He secluded himself and prayed until the rain came **(1 King 18:41-44)**.

Confessions are good. Declarations are great. All these things have their place, but the power you direct by confessing and declaring must have been made available from a long time of prayer. Don't get used to saying one or two words over a situation and saying it is done when it is apparent that nothing is done. Learn to stay on a matter until you tire out the enemy. Learn to persevere in the place of prayer.

In teaching about heartfelt and continued prayer, James says, "Elijah was a man with a nature just like us." He got tired. He got scared. He got discouraged. In spite of this, Elijah's persistence in prayer changed the weather. Friend, we may be people of like nature to Elijah, but if we will be people of like results, we must be people of like prayer.

3. IT'S AN INSTRUCTION.

The instruction to persevere in prayer is repeated too often to be ignored. Jesus taught it. We see this in **Luke 18:1** – "And he spake a parable unto them to this end, that men ought always to pray, and not to faint."

The word translated 'ought' actually means 'necessary'. Thus, Jesus is saying praying always is a necessity for men. Jesus is saying men must pray, without fainting. Learn not to tire easily. Learn not to gas out. Learn to pray always. Paul says the same in Colossians 4:2 – *"Continue in prayer, and watch in the same with thanksgiving."* This is the attitude of a man who perseveres in prayer: continuance. Continue in prayer. Don't stop. Keep going until you achieve your goal.

We see the same thought echoed in Ephesians 6:18 – "Praying always with all prayer and supplication in the Spirit, and watching thereunto with all perseverance and supplication for all saints." *Pray always.* Keep watch, not only for yourself, but persevere in prayer also for your brothers and sisters in Christ.

As I wrap up this chapter, I want you to remember one key thing: Continued prayer avails. Keep praying. God hears. God answers, and you will prevail. Just as the words of a popular hymn say:

O what peace we often forfeit
O what needless pain we bear
All because we do not carry everything to God in prayer

There are things God wants to do in your life. There are situations you need to change. The difference between where you are and where God will have you be is prayer. What can God achieve with your life if you wait on Him in the place of prayer? If all you needed to do to save your life was to pray a little longer, wouldn't you do it? Persevere in prayer, friend. Persevere.

Action Steps

Pick a particular matter or prayer point. Pray consistently and earnestly about it for seven days straight. Believe and trust that God hears and your prayer will prevail.

CHAPTER TEN
HYPERTROPHY IN PRAYER

xxxxxxxx

When I first started working out, I was going to the gym consistently without seeing results. I had fitness goals; I wanted to build muscle and I wanted to gain strength. However, I was definitely doing something wrong because it seemed like all my hardwork was for nothing. Until I got a personal trainer. He explained to me that there was a science to muscle building. For a muscle to grow, it must first die from exertion. The clinical term for this is *hypertrophy*. Muscle hypertrophy occurs when the fibres of the muscle sustain damage or injury, then the body repairs these muscle fibres by fusing them into bigger muscles.

Hypertrophy training is a controlled method of making your body build bigger muscles by tearing your already existing ones.

HYPERTROPHY IN PRAYER

To build muscle, you must lift weights that are heavy enough to tear your muscle fibres, and then force them to grow bigger. But you don't stop there; you keep lifting those heavy weights until you no longer feel the pain of exertion, and then you move on to heavier weights and begin the process again. By doing this, not only are you building bigger muscles, but those muscles are also developing strength.

So, what was happening with me? It's simple. Even though I was going to the gym consistently, the volume I was lifting was not sufficient to get my desired result. Hence, for muscle building and strength training in fitness, not only consistency matters, but volume also. You need both to achieve your desired result. Paul draws a parallel between spiritual devotions and exercise in his letter to Timothy.

> *"But reject profane and old wives' fables, and EXERCISE yourself toward godliness. For bodily exercise profits a little, but godliness is profitable for all things, having promise of the life that now is and of that which is to come."*
> **- 1 Timothy 4:7-8**

If you are familiar with how Paul used analogies to teach, you would understand that unless there was at least at the superficial level some similarity, he wouldn't use them. So, the reason he says, for instance, in **Ephesians 5:18,** "Do not be drunken with wine wherein is excess, but be filled with the Spirit," is because when you are full of the Spirit, there are some symptoms that are similar to the symptoms of drunkenness—incoherent speech, such as we have in tongues, and staggering.

In the same way, when Paul says, "Bodily exercise profits little," he's telling you there is an exercise in godliness. He literally says, "Exercise yourself rather unto godliness." It's an exercise, and so, the principles of exercise apply: Consistency and volume. Look at what Jesus said to His disciples at the Garden of Gethsemane:

> *"Then He came to the disciples and found them sleeping, and said to Peter, "What! Could you not watch with Me one hour?"*
> **- Matthew 26:40)**

This statement Jesus made teaches us something very important in prayer. "Couldn't you watch with me for one hour?" It means that although the disciples prayed, the prayer was not enough. It means volume matters. There is a time factor in prayer. The same

HYPERTROPHY IN PRAYER

way there is an estimated time for the food to be ready when you are cooking, time is also a factor when it comes to prayer. Just because food has been on the fire doesn't mean it is ready. You have to leave it on fire for the time period it needs to be done.

Don't let your prayer life become a farce, like those who go to the gym, pick up a few weights, take a few pictures for the 'gram, and then leave and never return. The true power of prayer is in the habits, not the action. Just like exercise, you won't see true results of prayer until you are doing the required volume, consistently.

What I'm trying to teach you is so simple, yet so powerful. In your prayer life, you must go for hypertrophy. Many men of God have tried to explain it to different generations in different ways. Kenneth Hagin calls it praying through—you pray until you hit a certain gusher. For this to happen, volume matters. Pray the required volume. Your spirit knows when a prayer is not enough. Obey the nudge and pray through. It may seem like your flesh is about to die, but you won't. You will hit that gusher where it seems like you are floating. You come out of the place of prayer and you go, "Where is the devil now?!" How about you create a prayer regimen and set a goal for yourself?

Prayer Has a Cumulative Effect

In **John 11:41-44**, Jesus stands before Lazarus' tomb and says, "Father, I thank you that you have heard me already." This should tell you something important: prayer has a cumulative effect. Jesus was invariably saying, "I have prayed to a certain extent, and I have come on the strength of my previous investments." He was saying, "Because you have heard me in my previous long prayer times, I thank you. Today I can make a short proclamation and Lazarus will come forth." Evidently, Jesus had prayed long so He could pray short.

The Bible teaches more on the *habit* of prayer than on the *action* of prayer. Prayer is a habit. Like velocity, it is measured over a period of time, not in an instant. There must be a consistency to it, a build-up. When Jude says, "Beloved building up yourselves on your most holy faith," it means that the more you stay, the more progress you make. You can rise up like an edifice in the place of prayer by building yourself up, brick upon brick. The more bricks you lay, the more progress you make.

This is why at the Garden of Gethsemane, Jesus could pray for a bit, take a minute, talk to the disciples, and go back to pray the same prayer point. He did that three times because the effect of prayer is cumulative. So, you don't pray until the time is up. You pray until that measure, that cumulative effect is accomplished.

HYPERTROPHY IN PRAYER

And when it's done, you say, "It's the time and the hour of darkness; let's go." That's the real secret in prayer; rising like an edifice with increasing volume and systematic consistency.

If you go to the gym consistently for two weeks and you have built strength to a particular level, if you do not keep at it, you will lose your progress. That muscle that you have built will atrophy from lack of use. When you finally return to the gym, you have to begin the process all over again, and the longer you have been away from the gym, the longer you have to work to build up strength to the level you were previously. So, regardless of how tired you get or how busy you get, you must keep at it to hit and sustain your fitness goals.

Once again, the heartfelt and continued prayer of a righteous man makes power available. So, if it is not heartfelt, if it is not continued, you are not going to have that cumulative effect. There must be consistency! If you pray today, you must pray tomorrow; otherwise, you will miss something.

Let the Giant in You Arise

"If you faint in the day of adversity, your strength is small."

- Proverbs 24:10

If the Bible says this, then it's true. If you faint in the day of adversity, it means your strength was not enough. You need to build more strength. Batteries have capacity at varying levels. However, the type of battery you purchase is dependent on the equipment you want to power. It's the same way in the realm of the Spirit, there is a measure that gets the job done.

Another analogy I would love to portray this with is the school grading system. For every report card you receive as a student, you do not fail because you scored a zero. Rather, to fail, there must be a certain cutoff mark you didn't meet. It could be 40%, 50%, or 60%, as the case may be. Meaning, if the cutoff mark is 60% and you score 59%, both you and the person who scored 0% would be graded 'failed'.

This principle sometimes applies in prayer as well. There is a measure that gets the work done. And so, like Peter, you might have prayed, but you have not prayed enough; therefore, when the test comes, you will not be prepared. So, spend more time praying. When you spend more time fanning the embers of your spirit, a giant can arise in you. A giant you never knew was lying there, waiting for an opportunity and the right structure. You will find yourself doing things you never thought you had the capacity to do. Listen, there are things that you might have been pushing against that have refused to move, but you are coming back with a force and an intensity that they never associated with you.

The same Peter whose life was plagued by weakness; of always over-promising and under-delivering, the same Peter stood before a crowd of more than three thousand and boldly declared the gospel. What changed?

> *"Tarry in the city of Jerusalem until you are endued with power from on high"*
> **- Luke 24:49**

That's the difference. Wait in prayer. Go for hypertrophy. Build strength, Build muscle. Let the giant in you arise!

Action Steps

I want to give you a challenge, a 50-day prayer challenge. Begin today; for 50 days, pray for at least one hour every day. Here is the recommended structure:

1 hour in the morning – 30 minutes in the afternoon – 1 hour at night. Do this consistently and religiously for 50 days.

CHAPTER ELEVEN

TONGUES PART 1:
WHY, WHAT AND WHOM

x x x x x x x x

There is no subject as unifying as prayer in the Body of Christ. Arguments may be endless on sacraments, generosity, healing, how to be saved, and even the doctrine of the Trinity. But almost unanimously, Christians pray, as they should. If there is anything the Church can come together to do without worrying about our differences, it will be to pray. But even prayer is not entirely exempt from controversy, specifically when it comes to spiritual gifts. Some people literally cringe the moment they hear "speaking in tongues." Our experiences and mental models have built a wall around our minds that even God is trying to reach over to get us to sit with the Word objectively. The words of Apostle Paul come to mind: *"Quench not the Spirit."* **- 1 Thessalonians 5:19**.

This means that there are things God wants to do in your life that you have the right to stop. You read right. He is all powerful, but has given you free will to accept or reject His provisions in your life. I sense that God wants to use this book to answer the questions of many on this subject. Would you at least study this objectively?

Why Is Speaking in Tongues Necessary?

1. **IT IS A CONFIRMATION OF THE TESTIMONY OF CHRIST.**

    You know why a lot of people are not interested in speaking in tongues? They do not understand its importance to begin with. For a lot of people, the tongues gift is just an addendum that some overzealous charismatics practise to make themselves feel better than others. This would explain their nonchalance about it. But the tongues gift is the most unique gift God gave the Church. Every other spiritual gift is not 'new'. Prophets of old prophesied, healed, and worked miracles. But the tongues gift could only be given to the Church because Jesus died, rose again, and ascended to the Father. The understanding of this changes everything! Follow the thought carefully.

When Peter was explaining what happened in the upper room, he said:

> *"This Jesus God has raised up, of which we are all witnesses. Therefore being exalted to the right hand of God, and having received from the Father the promise of the Holy Spirit, He poured out this which you now see and hear."*
>
> **–Acts 2:32-33**

Speaking in tongues is not a matter of denomination. It instead points to the resurrection of Jesus Christ! When you hear someone speak in tongues, that is proof that Jesus rose from the dead as He said He would! This is because the Holy Spirit could only be shed forth now that Jesus was glorified. Hence Peter saying, "...having received from the Father the promise of the Holy Spirit, He poured out this which you now see and hear." Yet, such a beautiful gift that displays the glorified Christ is misunderstood and constantly maligned. Paul repeated the same idea to the Church at Corinth when he said in **1 Corinthians 1:4-5**:

TONGUES PART 1: WHY, WHAT AND WHOM

"I thank my God always on your behalf, for the grace of God which is given you by Jesus Christ; that in every thing ye are enriched by him, in all utterance, and in all knowledge."

This right there is a sermon on its own. Some choose to be enriched by Christ in knowledge alone. Or just in sanctification, or faith, or generosity. But Paul says to be enriched also in utterance. Again this is not a denomination issue. It is God's Will that we all are enriched in divine utterance. What did Paul say next? Let's take a look at verses 6 and 7:

"Even as the testimony of Christ was confirmed in you: So that ye come behind in no gift; waiting for the coming of our Lord Jesus Christ."

Supernatural utterance is a confirmation of the testimony of Christ. When you see anyone speak in tongues, he is confirming that indeed Christ died, was buried, rose again, and ascended. This is huge! No one can truly understand this and be indifferent about speaking in tongues. My objective for this chapter is to help answer whatever questions you might have concerning the tongues gift, and to help you see clearly how necessary tongue-speaking is for every believer.

2. **IT CONFIRMS THE TESTIMONY OF THE BELIEVER**

It used to be a popular phrase for people to speak of being "born again with the evidence of speaking in tongues." People pushed back on that saying that there are a lot of genuinely saved people who do not speak in tongues, which is in fact true. But excesses of people aside, what does the Bible say about this?

Let's take a look at the story of Cornelius' conversion after Peter grudgingly went to preach the gospel to him. Peter's reluctance was due to the fact that, at the time, he and the other apostles did not believe that the Gentiles could be saved. But being compelled by a vision, Peter went to Cornelius' house where, as he grudgingly and religiously preached to Cornelius and his household, they were all filled with the Spirit and spoke with tongues.

Peter and those with him were astonished because they knew immediately what that meant. Cornelius speaking in tongues wasn't about denominationalism. It was an immediate witness that he and his household had been saved! Read it for yourself:

TONGUES PART 1: WHY, WHAT AND WHOM

> *"And those of the circumcision who believed were astonished, as many as came with Peter, because the gift of the Holy Spirit had been poured out on the Gentiles also."*
>
> **- Acts 10:45**

Well, how did they know?

> *"For they heard them speak with tongues and magnify God..."*
>
> **Acts 10:46 -**

This experience changed Peter's convictions immediately. He was convinced enough to explain to all the other Jews who criticised him for going to Cornelius' house in the first place. He recounted his experiences to these Jews in **Acts 11, verses 15-17**, saying: "And as I began to speak, the Holy Ghost fell on them as on us at the beginning. Then I remembered the word of the Lord, how that he said, John indeed baptised with water; but ye shall be baptised with the Holy Ghost. Forasmuch then as God gave them the like gift as he did unto us, who believed on the Lord Jesus Christ; what was I, that I could withstand God?"

Peter is basically saying, "The same phenomenon that authenticated our salvation, I saw in them. Regardless of my initial reluctance and reservations, when I heard them speak in tongues, I knew they were saved." Guess what? The fact that Cornelius and his house were filled with the Spirit ended all arguments for the Jews as well! We see this in verse 18: "When they heard these things they became silent; and they glorified God, saying, 'Then God has also granted to the Gentiles repentance to life.'"

Tongues-speaking confirms the testimony of the believer. While it is true that you can be born again and not speak in tongues because you were not taught, you cannot speak in tongues without being born again. Bear in mind that the witness of tongues was not independent of the fact that Cornelius believed the gospel. Cornelius believed and was filled with the Spirit demonstratively with the gift of tongues. If this story is anything to go by (and it is), it tells you that when a man like Cornelius honours God with his life, believes the gospel and speaks in tongues, it bears witness that he belongs to God's family.

3. **WHY NOT?**

I believe it takes a certain sense of pride for anyone to think they do not need tongues. How can God make a gift available to you and you insist you do not need it? Beloved, use ALL that God has given to you. **1 Corinthians 1:7** says, *"So that you come short in no gift, eagerly waiting for the revelation of our Lord Jesus Christ."*

If Paul lived in our day, he would have put it this way: "Don't sleep on this gift of tongues!." Or as Nigerians will say: "Don't dull." This is what Paul means when he says you should not come behind in any gift, especially as you wait for the coming of Christ. He says that because when Christ comes, no one will need a healing, a prophecy, or tongues and interpretation any more. Paul is saying in essence, use these gifts now! When Jesus said "These signs will follow you," it was because He knew you would need them! Do not try to insist otherwise. Jesus said "These signs shall follow them that believe. In my name, they shall speak with tongues…" Do you believe it? Well then, you should speak with tongues.

Dealing With the Misconceptions

1. <u>**SPEAKING IN TONGUES SHOULD NOT BE DONE TOGETHER/ALL AT THE SAME TIME**</u>

    You've probably heard people say, "What you see people do in these charismatic churches is wrong. They shouldn't all be speaking in tongues at the same time, because the Bible says in 1 Corinthians 14:27-28 that *"If any man speak in an unknown tongue, let it be by two, or at the most by three, and that by course; and let one interpret. But if there be no interpreter, let him keep silence in the church; and let him speak to himself, and to God.'"*

But the thing is, people who run off with this idea have failed to read that text in its proper context. Let's examine the preceding verses carefully:

> *"But now, brethren, if I come to you speaking with tongues, what shall I profit you unless I speak to you either by revelation, by knowledge, by prophesying, or by teaching?"*
> **- 1 Corinthians 14:6**

Why did Paul say, "If I come to you?" He said that because that's what they were doing! The Church at Corinth had, in their zeal, taken this spiritual language that should be used to communicate with God and started using it to speak to people to show off their spirituality. Without condemning that action outright, Paul says if you're going to do that, at least interpret. He tells them why in verse 16: *"Otherwise, if you bless with the spirit, how will he who occupies the place of the uninformed say 'Amen' at your giving of thanks, since he does not understand what you say?"*

TONGUES PART 1: WHY, WHAT AND WHOM

Let me give you a simple example. A lot of people prefer to pray to God in their native tongue when they are in private prayers. Your mother tongue helps you connect to God in a deep and personal way. But when leading a group in prayer, you are to either lead that prayer in a language everyone understands, or get an interpreter. That's common sense now, isn't it? Paul is addressing the rules of public prayer. That's why he is saying, if you speak in tongues and do not interpret, how will people say "amen" to your giving thanks?

Guess what? Even in a public meeting, as in many church services, there is time for personal prayers, where no one is leading and everyone just prays to God themselves. In this case, you need not worry about anyone's response because you are not talking to them! Paul is talking about leading a congregation in prayer and not a charismatic congregation praying in tongues. This is clear from the expressions "If I come to you," and "lest you say 'amen' when I give thanks."

It's funny that Paul still lets you know that even speaking to people in tongues is not wrong per se. Just like praying to God in your native language is not wrong. The problem is you won't be understood. Communication is the clear context here. Read on:

"I thank my God I speak with tongues more than you all; yet in the church I would rather speak five words with my understanding, that I may TEACH others also, than ten thousand words in a tongue."

- 1 Corinthians 14:17-18

Why does Paul say he would rather speak words people understand? That he may teach! This again proves that the context is addressing leading a church in prayer. In private prayers, the goal isn't to teach anyone. By the way, didn't you ever realise that EVERYWHERE a group of people were recorded to have prayed in tongues in the Bible, they did so together? Yes, the exact way some say it shouldn't be done. They did not take turns.

i. **The Upper Room** – *"And they were **all** filled with the Holy Spirit and began to speak with other tongues, as the Spirit gave them utterance."* **(Acts 2:4)** There was such a commotion that it drew a crowd. Note that had it been one of two people speaking, no crowd would have shown up wondering what was happening. When the crowd gathered (verse 7), they said: *"Look, are not **all these** who speak Galileans?" Everyone was speaking!*

TONGUES PART 1: WHY, WHAT AND WHOM

ii. **Cornelius' House** – *"For they heard them speak with tongues and magnify God."* **(Acts 10:46);** Acts 19:6 – *"And when Paul had laid hands on them, the Holy Spirit came upon them, and they spoke with tongues and prophesied."*

Clearly, a congregation praying in tongues was not strange in the Bible. So again, what then was Paul referring to? Leading prayers or teaching in tongues. The latter part of that chapter makes this clear as day. He says: *"How is it then, brethren? Whenever you come together, each of you has a psalm, has a teaching, has a tongue, has a revelation, has an interpretation. Let all things be done for edification."* **- 1 Corinthians 14:26)**

Think about it this way. In every church, there are people who can sing that aren't in the choir. But in church, we cannot all sing except we are called upon to do so. When it comes to leading the congregation, things must be done in an orderly manner and to carry everyone along. So, the principle here doesn't apply only to speaking in tongues. This verse clearly shows the rule applies to psalms, revelations, and teaching. You might be a great teacher, but if you're not the one to teach in church that day, you keep quiet. If you're not the one to lead a song that day, you keep quiet. When it comes to addressing the congregation, too many people at a time becomes chaotic. Hence Paul saying:

> *"If anyone speaks in a tongue, let there be two or at the most three, each in turn, and let one interpret."*
> **−1 Corinthians 14:27**

This doesn't mean, however, that you cannot sing to yourself and to God in time of personal supplication in the same church. See what Paul says next in verse 28:

> *"But if there is no interpreter, let him keep silent in church, and let him speak to himself and to God."*

What are you to do if there is no interpreter? Shut up altogether? No. He says speak to yourself and to God. You and everyone else are free to speak to God in tongues. You do not have to bother about interpreting when you are not addressing or disturbing the congregation. When you speak in tongues, God understands what you are saying.

2. **NOT EVERYONE CAN SPEAK IN TONGUES**

Once upon a time, in the Old Testament, only few people could have the Spirit upon them; Kings, judges, priests, prophets and people with special duties. But Moses made a profound statement: *"Then Moses said to him, "Oh, that all the*

TONGUES PART 1: WHY, WHAT AND WHOM

Lord's people were prophets and that the Lord would put His Spirit upon them!" **- Numbers 11:29**

How lavish it would be, that God will put his Spirit upon all men. Would that ever happen? Centuries after, Joel prophesied: *"And it shall come to pass afterward that I will pour out My Spirit on all flesh; your sons and your daughters shall prophesy, your old men shall dream dreams, your young men shall see visions. And also on My menservants and on My maidservants I will pour out My Spirit in those days."* **- Joel 2:28-29**

God, through the prophet Joel, promised to pour out his spirit on ALL flesh. To emphasise that no one will be left out, He used poetic examples of sons and daughters (no gender restrictions), old and young (no age restrictions) servants and handmaidens (no class restrictions). Everyone will function in the gifts of the Spirit. This prophecy was fulfilled on the Day of Pentecost, where all 120 people were filled with the Spirit and spoke in tongues. Every single one of them. Peter, commenting on this said: *"This is what the prophet Joel prophesied."* **- Acts 2:16**.

Friend, bear in mind that the Spirit of God working with people was not new to the Jews. They had prophets of old who were filled with the Spirit. What makes the promise of the Spirit in the New Testament unique is that it is for ALL. When people suggest otherwise, they tamper with the very fabric and glory of the New Testament's promise. Everyone in the New Testament who believed in Jesus and desired to be filled with the Spirit was filled with the Spirit. When you see anyone suggest that the gifts aren't for everyone, understand that there is no single biblical evidence of that. Everywhere the spirit fell, He fell on **all** who believed, just as God said He would.

When the elite Cornelius was being filled, his servants and entire household were filled as well (Acts 10:44-46). Do you know what proves more than anything that the tongues gift is for every believer? It is this text: *"And when Simon saw that through the laying on of the apostles' hands the Holy Spirit was given, he offered them money, saying, 'Give me this power also, that anyone on whom I lay hands may receive the Holy Spirit.'"* – **Acts 8:18-19.**

It was clear to even this greedy, unregenerate sorcerer that everyone the apostles laid their hands on were filled with the Spirit. This man was wrong and silly to have tried to offer money for it, but the fact that he did proves that he saw it as something predictable. No one offers money for something that may not work or only works once in a while.

TONGUES PART 1: WHY, WHAT AND WHOM

But everyone in Samaria that believed and had hands laid on them were filled with the Spirit. It is for everyone! Quit doubting and believe the words of Jesus. It is for you! It is for today!

3. TONGUES IS HUMAN LANGUAGES

"Cretans and Arabs—we hear them speaking in our own tongues the wonderful works of God."

- Acts 2:11

The misconception that the gift of tongues is human languages comes from a faulty understanding of this verse of scripture above. However, Paul, in 1 Corinthians 14:2 clearly tells us this: *"For he that speaketh in an unknown tongue speaketh not unto men, but unto God: for no man understandeth him; howbeit in the spirit he speaketh mysteries."*

Look at that! Clear as day. When a person speaks in tongues NO ONE understands him. When you speak with tongues, you speak in a language no man in his normal faculty can interpret or understand. So, it is either Paul the apostle is wrong, or our understanding of Acts 2 is wrong.

A lot of people say that the tongues gift is the Spirit of God enabling you to speak a human language you never learnt so you can evangelise the natives of that language. But here are the reasons that cannot be true: There is no such example in the Bible. Nowhere did the apostles go to preach to people and supernaturally spoke a language they never learnt, and that the people natively spoke. On the contrary, in every place speaking in tongues was done, it was amongst people who already spoke the native language. In Cornelius' house for instance, Peter could already communicate with Cornelius. The tongues gift was not therefore given to aid communication or evangelism. If speaking in tongues was done in human languages, then it means interpretation is not a gift (and it is). Both tongues and interpretation of tongues are gifts of the Spirit. The Bible says: *"...to another different kinds of tongues, to another the interpretation of tongues."* **(1 Corinthians 12:10)**. If you ever speak a language that people do not need the Spirit to understand, you did not speak in tongues. Interpretation itself is a gift, which is why Paul says *"Let he that speaks in tongues pray that he may interpret."* **(1 Corinthians 14:13)**. By the way, people who hold to these views are often found contradicting themselves without even knowing it. They, on one hand, insist that you shouldn't speak in tongues unless there's an interpreter, and then on the other hand insist that speaking in tongues is speaking a language the natives of any given country

TONGUES PART 1: WHY, WHAT AND WHOM

understand. But if I travel to China and speak Mandarin even if I never learnt the language, and I'm therefore able to preach the gospel in China, I would not need an interpreter for the Chinese to understand Mandarin. Read this objectively to see what Paul says will happen if people who know nothing about tongues hear you speak in tongues: *"Therefore if the whole church comes together in one place, and all speak with tongues, and there come in those who are uninformed or unbelievers, will they not say that you are out of your mind?"* **(1 Corinthians 14:23)**. Why would they say you are out of your mind if you are speaking their language? They'd say you are out of your mind because speaking in tongues actually sounds like gibberish to the natural man. It is not human language.

> *"Therefore, if I do not know the meaning of the language, I shall be a foreigner to him who speaks, and he who speaks will be a foreigner to me."*
>
> **- 1 Corinthians 14:11**

Some also have the notion that there are both tongues in human languages and tongues of angels because of the text that says, *"Though I speak with the tongues of men and of angels, but have not love, I have become sounding brass or a clanging cymbal."* **(1 Corinthians 13:1)** But here, Paul was simply using a figure of speech called hyperbole. Just like one saying: "Even if your son were as tall as Mount Everest, we won't let him join the team." Paul continued the idea through to the third verse when he said: "And though I bestow all my goods to feed *the poor*, and though I give my body to be burned, but have not love, it profits me nothing." **- 1 Corinthians 13:3**

Most people will never do these, but Paul said that to emphasise the futility of the most generous acts not done in love. If tongues of angels was something to know and do, we'd read about it in other texts. You don't base your theology off one statement made as a clear illustration. So, what then happened in Acts 2?

Before I share my thoughts on this, let me paint you a picture. Imagine you were a student, and you missed a class and had to attend a revision class to go over what was taught. This revision class is important to prepare you for exams you are to write the next day. However, two different revision classes are being held concurrently, one hosted by the best student in your class, and the other by the lecturer himself. Imagine you choose to attend both classes just to be extra prepared, but to your surprise, both classes seem to have taught varying things on the subject. Whose teaching will you trust in preparation for the examination? Of course the lecturer's! Why? Because he has authority.

TONGUES PART 1: WHY, WHAT AND WHOM

In our context, the two seemingly different views (although not different) on tongues are Acts 2 and in 1 Corinthians 14. Acts 2 is an account of people who, although they did not speak in tongues themselves, heard people speak in tongues. 1 Corinthians 14 is a detailed teaching of an apostle on the gift of tongues. Experiences such as you have in Acts 2, though sincere, can be a bit subjective, but a teaching is authoritative. This is why you use 1 Corinthians 14 to help you understand Acts 2, not the other way around.

A lot of things do not quite check out when you read Acts 2 at face value. There is more to the story. Put on your thinking caps and let's examine this together: What gathered the crowd? If you had a friend who could speak Spanish and you didn't know, how's that so astonishing? I mean, you'd probably say, "How come you never told me?," wait for an explanation, and eventually move on. There is nothing quite astonishing about 120 people speaking your language. It might catch their attention, but it is highly unlikely that thousands of people would gather at your doorstep just because they heard their language being spoken. I'm not saying it didn't happen. I'm saying there is clearly more to the story. If a hundred and twenty people prayed at the same time, you wouldn't hear any of them. Anyone who went to school knows this. Remember those times the lecturer stepped out of the class and everyone began to make noise? If you stayed outside to eavesdrop, which one particular student would you hear? None!

All you would hear is noise. If a multitude gathered outside the upper room, calling in to have heard everyone up there in their own language, there is more to the story. How come some people accused the disciples in the upper room of being drunk? There is nothing "drunk" about 120 people praying in your language. There's more to the story.

The explanation:

So, what do we really make of the Acts 2 story? I'd give you a short answer, and then a slightly longer one. Read carefully. The crowd puzzled this: "And how *is it that* we hear, each in our own language in which we were born?" **- Acts 2:8**

Did it ever occur to you that the Bible never said the folks in the upper room spoke in their native languages? It simply said they spoke in tongues. But every one of the witnesses heard it in his/her mother tongue. Note that this isn't the interpretation of tongues. It is simply a one-off miracle. In case you are doubting the possibility of this being the cause, understand that it had happened before.

Understanding The Pentecost

What was The Pentecost really about? The Pentecost was a Jewish celebration that was held fifty days after the Passover. It was to

TONGUES PART 1: WHY, WHAT AND WHOM

commemorate the giving of the law. The Passover was, on the other hand, a Jewish feast to commemorate the children of Israel being freed from Egypt. Through both feasts, God was showing in a prophetic parable what He was going to do in Christ. Christ is our Passover. The Bible says that in 1 Corinthians 5:7. Just the same way the angel of death saw the blood and passed over the houses of the Jews, when we believe in Jesus, His blood sets us free from death and eternal judgement.Now, about The Pentecost, do you not see the similarities between the giving of the Spirit and the giving of the law? When the law was given on Mount Sinai, the following happened: There was a sound. People heard trumpets on Mount sinai. It was a supernatural occurrence. In Acts 2, there was a sound. too. This time, a rushing mighty wind. There was fire from the mountain. In Acts 2, cloven tongues as of fire sat on the head of everyone:

> *"And Moses brought the people out of the camp to meet with God, and they stood at the foot of the mountain. Now Mount Sinai was completely in smoke, because the LORD descended upon it in fire. Its smoke ascended like the smoke of a furnace, and the whole mountain quaked greatly. And*

> *when the blast of the trumpet sounded long and became louder and louder, Moses spoke, and God answered him by voice."*
>
> **- Exodus 19:17-19**

At Mount Sinai, about 3000 men died. On the Day of Pentecost, about 3000 souls were saved! **(Exodus 32:28, Acts 2:41)**. According to Jewish tradition, when God spoke from the mountain, everyone heard him in their own tongue. First century rabbi, Rabbi Yochanan says that the voice of God was split to seventy languages. Matching the languages among the seventy nations.

Basically, the same way The Passover was to foreshadow Christ and His redemptive work, The Pentecost was to foreshadow the Advent of the Spirit. God ensured there would be similarities, so that the people would know that these things happened in fulfilment of His promise to the Jews. Also, the events happened on the exact anniversaries of The Passover and The Pentecost. This is what happened in the upper room.

What Is Speaking in Tongues

Speaking in tongues is a unique and personal spiritual language through which the spirit of the believer communicates with God in a way that sounds like gibberish to the natural man. That

TONGUES PART 1: WHY, WHAT AND WHOM

praying in the Spirit is a unique language is not something you can wiggle around. It is clear in the scriptures. Paul says: "For if I pray in an *unknown* tongue, my spirit prayeth, but my understanding is unfruitful. What is it then? I will pray with the spirit, and I will pray with the understanding also: I will sing with the spirit, and I will sing with the understanding also." **(1 Corinthians 14:15)**

This means, when you pray in the Spirit, your mind does not understand what you are saying. As such there is a need for interpretation. You would need to pray in the Spirit and also in your understanding. This is why some observers described the disciples as being drunk in **Acts 2:13:** *"Others mocking said, 'They are full of new wine.'"*

Two main things characterise a drunk person: incoherent speech and staggering. What similarities does tongue-speaking bear with drunkeness? There is no way the observers heard the disciples speak articulately in the language they understood and concluded the disciples were drunk. There must have been a sway between languages. They supernaturally could understand what they might have referred to as gibberish. By the way, you should find it interesting that Paul also makes this comparison in Ephesians 5:18 – "And do not be drunk with wine, in which is dissipation; but be filled with the Spirit,." Why did Paul make this comparison? Your guess is as good as mine.

1 Corinthians 14:2 also says, *"For he that speaketh in an unknown tongue speaketh not unto men, but unto God: for no man understandeth him; howbeit in the spirit he speaketh mysteries."*

Look at that! Mysteries! Tongues is encoded language! When you speak with tongues, you speak in a language no one in their normal faculty can interpret or understand. Incoherent speech! Yes, it might sound like rubbish to your natural mind, but God sees it as a communication channel between your spirit and His. You are communicating a mystery in your spirit unto God. If it doesn't make sense, it means you are getting it right. Your understanding must be unfruitful for it to be tongues!

There are two main ways by which you identify a drunk person. Their speech is slurred; incoherent. They often stagger. Some even fall down. Does this sound familiar? Have you ever experienced or observed this? When it looks like the worship is going on and everything is nice, all of a sudden, your legs are feeling light and you stagger or even fall. The infilling of the Spirit gives this effect!

In Peter's response in Acts 2:33, he says, "Therefore being by the right hand of God exalted and having received of the Father the promise of the Holy Ghost, he had shed forth this, which you now see and hear."

TONGUES PART 1: WHY, WHAT AND WHOM

So, on that day, the observers perceived the event both by seeing and by hearing. They heard incoherent speech and they saw people staggering. As a result, they came to the conclusion that the apostles were drunk. Friends, as long as it is biblical, "strange" is okay. Do not quench the move of the Spirit in your life. The fact that tongues may not look cool doesn't mean that it won't change your life. God loves you and gave you this gift. Embrace it!

CHAPTER TWELVE

TONGUES PART 2:
HOW TO SPEAK IN TONGUES

×××××××××

For those who have read and understood all that has been said about tongues and want to be filled with the Spirit, this is for you. This chapter is to walk you through the process of being filled with the Spirit and speaking in tongues. I want to get you filled with the Spirit if you have never been. "Through a book?," you might ask. Well, yes. Just as the Spirit is not limited by distance, He is also not limited by any medium. If healings can happen via articles of clothing as in **Acts 19:12**, the supernatural can be transferred via a book. Just believe. You will be filled with the Spirit.

TONGUES PART 2: HOW TO SPEAK IN TONGUES

I will begin with a bold statement that is proven beyond reasonable doubt through biblical accounts: It is impossible for a believer to desire the infilling of the Spirit and be denied. You cannot present the truth about the infilling of the Spirit to a person and then he/she earnestly and sincerely desires it, but God then withholds it. It has never happened and it will never happen. If there was any situation where you thought it happened, it was either that the subject of the infilling was not properly taught, and so the person who was desiring it received it, but didn't know that he/she had received it.

For instance, if you are wrongly taught that tongues-speaking is in human language, you are not going to speak in tongues. Or If you are wrongly taught that in speaking with tongues, the Holy Spirit will come from inside you, hold your tongue and start wagging it, you will keep waiting for that to happen. The only hindrance is wrong teaching. The truth about the infilling of the Spirit can never be presented to a believer who sincerely and earnestly desires it yet doesn't receive it. There is no biblical example for that.

In **Luke 11:11-13**, Jesus says "If a son asks for bread from any father among you, will he give him a stone? Or if *he asks* for a fish, will he give him a serpent instead of a fish? Or if he asks for an egg, will he offer him a scorpion? If you then, being evil, know how to give good gifts to your children, how much more will *your* heavenly Father give the Holy Spirit to those who ask Him!"

Jesus uses an analogy about biological fathers to teach you about the heavenly Father. He's letting you know how ridiculous it is for you to think you will ask for the Holy Spirit and not receive Him. If you then, in your normal human fallen states, still know how to do good for your children, how much more your heavenly Father? This is the heavenly Father; He surpasses you in kindness and goodness! If you are not filled with the Spirit, you need to know without an iota of doubt that if you would ask today, you will be filled. If you ask, you will be filled. This applies to every single person. It's not possible for you to ask and not be filled.

Are You Thirsty?

There were two categories of people in Jesus' earthly ministry. There was a class of people whom He marvelled at their unbelief, and there was another class of people whom He marvelled at their faith. Jesus preached to the Jews often and it looked like He struggled to convince them. Yet on two different occasions, Jesus commended the faith of two different people—the Syrophoenician woman and the centurion.

The centurion came to Jesus, saying, "I have a servant at home who is sick." Jesus, because of His everyday dealings with people

TONGUES PART 2: HOW TO SPEAK IN TONGUES

who didn't have so great a faith, says, "Okay, I'm coming to your house." The centurion then replies, saying: "What do you mean, you're coming, sir? I'm a man under authority; I say to a servant, 'Go,' and he goes. To another one, 'Come,' and he comes. Speak the word only."

Jesus marvelled at this response. He had never seen anybody exhibit so great a faith. At least not in Israel. You may want to go meet the Roman centurion and ask, "How did you get your faith to this level? Because, you know, I've been going to different faith clinics, reading a lot of books; you know, exercising my faith. Meanwhile yours just comes effortlessly."

Well, the centurion didn't read any books or attend any special meetings. He didn't need to. The reason is because in the fabric of every human being, you will find faith. Faith is our norm. It is unbelief that is the anomaly. If you see anybody who struggles to believe, he/she has done something to themselves. The natural man thirsts after God. Paul described it this way in **Romans 1:20**. He says, *"The invisible things about God are clearly seen in the things that he has created. So man is without excuse."*

When we observe the Earth; how it functions; its beauty, the precision and the intelligence in its design, it awakens in us the desire to believe in a creator. It compels us to search for God. In

John 7:37, on the last day, the great day of the feast, Jesus stood and cried with a loud voice saying, "If any man thirst, let him come to me and drink."

God doesn't offer hunger. He doesn't make people thirsty. Man thirsts, God offers water. If anyone does not thirst, then something is wrong. He/she had the capacity to, but must have suppressed that thirst **(Romans 1:21-23)**.

There are three examples that can attest to this. Think of the Ethiopian eunuch, Cornelius, and the Samaritan woman. All three of these people were already looking for God before God found them. When Philip, by the leading of the Spirit came close to the Ethiopian eunuch's chariot, what did Philip see the man doing? He was reading the book of Isaiah! He wanted to know! There was a curiosity in the eunuch's heart. The Lord saw this and worked a miracle. He brought a man of God to explain.

For Cornelius, no one had yet preached to him, but the Bible says he was a devout and generous man. He and all his household knew there was a God out there. They didn't really know what He was like or even know His name, but the little they knew caused them to live with a level of consciousness. God saw this and intervened. An angel appears to Cornelius and says, "Send for a man named Peter, he will tell you what, by which you will be saved."

TONGUES PART 2: HOW TO SPEAK IN TONGUES

The third but not so obvious example is the Samaritan woman. Most times, it is her scandal that gets our attention—the fact that she had five husbands and a concubine, but the most important aspect of the story is her hunger for the knowledge of God. She meets someone for the first time. She doesn't know who He is. However, through His display of prophetic gifts, she figures out He is a prophet of some sort. Finally, this was her opportunity to ask some pertinent Bible questions.

The woman had been studying, she had questions, and she had been looking for someone who had the answers. It was top of mind. And so, even though it was a little uncomfortable; a stranger telling her about her marital history, the Samaritan woman was not going to miss the opportunity to ask her questions. She then went on to ask about the right place to worship, a controversial question between the Jews and the gentiles. Jesus explained, but the woman wasn't really convinced and she didn't want to be rude. So, she replied, "Anyway, the Messiah is coming."

Look at that! She was anticipating the Messiah! This woman knew all her Bible questions would be answered when the Messiah came. This same Jesus who had been trying to teach the Jews, here was a Samaritan woman, eagerly awaiting His coming. It was her thirst that made Jesus sit on that well.

What does this have to do with a teaching on tongues? Everything! In every genuine spiritual experience, you and God will meet halfway. When it comes to a teaching on tongues, even the best eisegesis requires hunger (desire). If your doubt is strong enough, it will still excuse you from the best arguments.

The Parable of the Sower teaches us that spiritual impact is not always about the efficacy of the word. As viable as a seed is, it must land in the right place! It won't grow in your cup, it won't grow in the plate, or grow on tiles. If you put the seed in stony places, it might germinate but not thrive. If you put it among thorns, it will thrive but for a while. For a seed to take root and bloom, it must be planted in good, fertile ground. So, it is not just about how great the teaching is, how great the word is, or how great the explanation is. It is about your heart! What is the condition of your heart? What is the receptiveness of your heart?

1 Corinthians 14:1a says, *"Pursue love, and desire spiritual gifts."* It is an instruction to desire spiritual gifts. The KJV translation of **1 Corinthians 12:31** says *covet earnestly*. You must yearn to desire spiritual gifts. You must display a hunger for the things of the Spirit. Speaking in tongues is the easiest thing for a hungry person. Some of the arguments against tongues are so silly. "Tongues-speaking is not for everybody." How they came about that theory should not even bother you. Even if the gift of tongues was not for everybody, why must you excuse yourself? It's not a doctrine problem but a thirst problem. If there were only five slots for tongues, then one must belong to you. That's what made the Syrophoenician woman a woman of great faith. Jesus was not going to budge. He even tried to discourage her saying, "It is not for me to give food that is meant for children to dogs." However, instead of getting angry, the woman insisted on getting what she wanted.

Great faith does not tolerate excuses, and when it comes to the things of the Spirit, that's the mentality you must have. There must be a yearning, a true desire from your heart to be included. You must have the curiosity of Peter when he saw Jesus walking on water. Peter told Jesus to ask him to come if truly He was the one. You must have that type of curiosity. You must be ready to try. You must dare to believe the Word of God. You must have childlike faith! Childlike faith is all it takes for a hungry person who believes **(Mark 16:17)** to speak with tongues. It is doubt that makes you need so much corroboration.

You Must Be Born Again

The incident at the upper room at The Pentecost was an evidence of the fulfilment of a promise Jesus made to His disciples; the promise of the Holy Spirit. In **John 14:16-17**, Jesus speaking, said:

"And I will pray the Father, and He will give you another Helper, that He may abide with you forever—the Spirit of truth, whom the world cannot receive, because it neither sees Him nor knows Him; but you know Him, for He dwells with you and will be in you."

And when Peter stands to address the crowd in **Acts 2:33**, He says, *"Therefore being exalted to the right hand of God, and having received from the Father the promise of the Holy Spirit, He poured out this which you now see and hear."* He is stating explicitly that the manifestation which the crowd witnessed was evidence that Jesus had received and given the promised Holy Spirit. Tongues-speaking is a spiritual utterance possible to only those who have the Spirit **(1 Corinthians 12:7 & 10)**.

How then do you receive the Holy Spirit? Ephesians 1:13 says, "In Him you also *trusted,* after you heard the word of truth, the gospel of your salvation; in whom also, having believed, you were sealed with the Holy Spirit of promise." The Holy Spirit is the seal of salvation given to all who believe in Jesus. This is why Jesus said, "These signs shall follow them that believe. In my name … they shall speak in new tongues." Once you believe in Jesus, you receive the Holy Spirit, and then, you can speak in tongues. Hence, if you are not born again—if you have not received the gift of salvation in Christ Jesus—you must do so before you can speak in tongues.

TONGUES PART 2: HOW TO SPEAK IN TONGUES

If you need more information about this, you can read my book, *Saving Grace*, or listen to any sermon on the gospel.

FOUR THINGS TO NOTE BEFORE SPEAKING IN TONGUES.

1. **Get your mind out of the way**: Don't let your intellect be a hindrance. The Bible gives you a heads-up in 1 Corinthians 14 that your understanding will be unfruitful. It's going to sound like rubbish to your mind; you read that from the Word of God. The only witness you're going to get is from within. You will be edified as you do it even more.

2. **You are the one to speak**: Understand that nobody will speak in tongues for you. The Holy Spirit won't shake your vocal chords for tongues to come out. Acts 2:4 says, "And they were all filled with the Holy Ghost, and began to speak with other tongues, as the Spirit gave them utterance." You have control over it, just like a natural language. The spirit of the prophet is subject to the prophet. It is subject to you! If it is involuntary, it is most likely a demon! The Holy Spirit is not going to grip you and force your mouth to move. What the Holy Spirit does is He gives the utterance. That is, when you open your mouth in faith and boldness, there is a flow that is not premeditated. However, it begins with you taking the step and speaking. For some, it is dramatic, while in some

others it is not. There is a faith dimension to it. But you have to speak.

3. **You cannot go wrong**: When it comes to tongues, understand that you cannot go wrong. There is no biblical precedence for false tongues. If we won't give a stone to our child who asks for bread, how much more God? Don't worry about not sounding the way someone else does. They might have been doing it for decades. So, even if yours is monosyllabic or two words only, it does not make what you're doing illegitimate. You express it in faith because Jesus said if you ask, you will receive **(John 7:37-39)**.

The gift of tongues comes with the Advent of the Spirit. If you are born again, you already have the Spirit in you. So, what happens when you begin to pray in tongues? It is just a stir of what you already have, and sometimes, all you need is just understanding because in the realm of the Spirit, it is possible to have something for long and not know.

Peter had been a fisherman all throughout his career, yet to walk on water had never occurred to him until he saw someone else do it; until he had the invitation to come. And just like we established early on, God and man must meet halfway. Jesus did not carry Peter from the boat just because Peter wanted to walk

TONGUES PART 2: HOW TO SPEAK IN TONGUES

on water. Peter himself took steps of faith out of the boat. So, the problem is not supply, the problem is you have not approached. The invitation is there to come. Peter got up and that's what we are meant to do. You're going to release your faith and speak. You're going to flow with it. If you want it, drink.

Action Steps

If you have never spoken in tongues before, you can do so now. Say this:

Jesus said the sign of new tongues follows all who believe in His name. I believe. I have the Holy Spirit. Right now, I am full of the Spirit, from the crown of my head to the tips of my toes. Out of my belly flows rivers of living water. I've got it, and in the name of Jesus, I put my doubt out of the way. I speak in tongues!

Now begin to speak.

Pray in tongues without an agenda for at least 15 minutes every day.

CHAPTER THIRTEEN
GAINING BACK SPIRITUAL FORM

××××××××

After watching some action movies, the typical young child might go out into their neighbourhood and try to imitate what they have seen. At some point in your life, you probably wished that you could run as fast as The Flash, fly like Superman, or climb walls like Spider-Man. While we know that there are no superheroes in the world, have you observed that for most of the things you see in the movies as fiction, the Bible has true stories of people who have done them. Elijah outran a chariot, Samson carried the gate of a city up a hill, Peter walked on water, and Moses parted the Red Sea. So, maybe there actually are superheroes today, and you, dear believer, are one of them.

There's something else we learn from superhero movies. We learn that as great as the capabilities that these superheroes had were, there were certain circumstances in which those capabilities were inhibited. For Superman, for instance, it was kryptonite. As powerful as Superman is, when kryptonite shows up, he will be weakened. The same goes for believers. There are circumstances or environments that a believer finds himself in that will not allow his capabilities to find full expression. Let us examine a couple:

1. IGNORANCE

Almost every single prayer of the apostle Paul for the Church in the New Testament was for them to grow in the knowledge of all that they now had in Christ. To the Ephesian church, he says:

> *"The eyes of your understanding being enlightened; that you may know what is the hope of His calling, what are the riches of the glory of His inheritance in the saints."*
> **-Ephesians 1:18**

In like manner, Paul prayed for the church in Colossae, saying:

> *"For this reason we also, since the day we heard it, do not cease to pray for you, and to ask that you may be filled with the knowledge of His will in all wisdom and spiritual understanding."*
> **- Colossians 1:9**

This goes to show that the importance of the believer knowing and growing in the knowledge of what he/she has cannot be overemphasised, because if you don't know what you have, it won't matter what you have.

There are several misconceptions out there about prayer. For example, some believe that it is the duty of the spirit to always stir us to pray; hence, they only pray when they "feel" like praying. Well, if you only pray when you feel like praying, you will never have a prayer life. The responsibility to constantly put fire on your prayer altar is yours. A good analogy for this is the instruction given to the Levitical priesthood concerning the fire on the altar for the burnt offering:

> *"And the fire on the altar shall be kept burning on it; it shall not be put out. And the priest shall burn wood on it every morning, and lay the burnt offering in order on it; and he shall burn on it the fat of the peace offerings."*
> **– Leviticus 6:12**

God was not the one to keep the fire burning, it was the priest. This is the same instruction we have been given:

GAINING BACK SPIRITUAL FORM

"Do not be slothful in zeal, be fervent in spirit, serve the Lord. Rejoice in hope, be patient in tribulation, be constant in prayer."

- Romans 12:11-12, ESV

You are the one who will not be slothful in zeal. You have that responsibility to put fire on your altar. Being fervent in the spirit is an instruction. How do you achieve that? Paul tells you in verse 12: *"Be constant in prayer."*

1. WEIGHTS

"Therefore we also, since we are surrounded by so great a cloud of witnesses, let us lay aside every weight, and the sin which so easily ensnares us, and let us run with endurance the race that is set before us."

–Hebrews 12:1

'Weight' here is a metaphor. In the context of the scripture above, it refers to unbelief. The writer of Hebrews was writing to Jews not to reject the message of the gospel. However, *weight* can also be used in a general sense to refer to other sins, not just unbelief. And so, the writer lets you know that when you're in a race, the last thing you want to do is carry weights.

So, in your walk of spiritual devotions, there are things such as habits that can hinder you from going as far as you should. This varies from person to person. For Esau, it was food; for Judas, it was money; for Samson, it was women. Consistently accommodating contradictions will hinder you from running as you ought to. It has stopped many mighty men.

FIVE ACTIONS TO TAKE TO RESTORE SPIRITUAL FORM

1. **SIGHT**

   In the body of Christ, we learn by seeing. There are some things you are not taught. You just need to see them repeatedly. Anything you see repeatedly, you will end up doing. A lot of people underestimate the power of association. If all your friends are not prayerful, they don't study the Bible, and they never bring up Jesus in their conversations, it's not a prophecy of doom, but you're most likely going to be like them.

   When Saul found himself in the company of prophets, he prophesied. The event was so significant that the people began to ask, "Is Saul a prophet also?" Another example we see is the story of Peter and Jesus. Peter sees Jesus walking on water and says, "I want to join you," and he did. This is what

GAINING BACK SPIRITUAL FORM

it takes to be a doer of God's word. The apostle James, in a letter to the Church, says:

> *"But be doers of the word, and not hearers only, deceiving yourselves. For if anyone is a hearer of the word and not a doer, he is like a man observing his natural face in a mirror; for he observes himself, goes away, and immediately forgets what kind of man he was. But he who looks into the perfect law of liberty and continues in it, and is not a forgetful hearer but a doer of the work, this one will be blessed in what he does."*
>
> **- James 1:22-25**

It says that's what it takes to be a doer, because if you see the right things, recollect the right things, you will do the right things. Yes, you don't feel like praying, but do you belong to a praying church? Do you have praying friends? When was the last time you read a spiritual book? When was the last time you listened to a sermon? You have to be intentional about feeding your spirit through what you see.

2. **EFFORT**

When it comes to showing effort in spiritual things, a good example I love to use is the way we put effort into succeeding academically. The mere fact that you have passed an exam in school before is a testament to the fact that you can be doing better in your spiritual life.

In your preparation for exams, you don't just say, "Oh, I don't feel like reading, so you don't read. When you don't feel like reading, you go the extra mile; you stand up, pace the room. Sometimes, you take extreme measures, such as putting your legs inside a bucket of water. You have to be willing to put in even much more effort when it comes to spiritual things.

3. **EMPHASIS**

When you are trying to overcome your lack of interest in something, you do it repeatedly. So, when I don't feel like praying, I'm going to pray until I stop feeling like not praying. Someone once said to me, "Pastor, I've not been praying. What do I do?" I replied, saying " Have you prayed about it?"

When you don't feel like praying, get to praying anyway. Sometimes, you have to throw it beyond the mark to make up for the lack of interest. You go on a prayer journey. You create emphasis for yourself. Have a special season of devotional emphasis. You can go on a sermon diet of only listening to sermons on prayer. The key is to emphasise what you want to see in your life.

4. **ACCOUNTABILITY**

This is another very powerful method to regain your spiritual form. As a Body, we all need each other. Even a pastor is fed by feeding. Paul, in his letter to the Church in Rome said:

> *"For I long to see you, that I may impart to you some spiritual gift, so that you may be established— that is, that I may be encouraged together with you by the mutual faith both of you and me."*
>
> **- Romans 1:11-12**

So yes, I am coming to Rome to impart unto you some spiritual gifts, but in doing so, I also will benefit from the warmth of fellowship. If you are too individualistic in your approach, you will struggle. Get yourself a prayer partner, even if only temporarily for the duration in which you are working to get your prayer life back on track.

> *"As iron sharpens iron, so a man sharpens the countenance of his friend."*
>
> **- Proverbs 27:17**

Some of us have friend mentors who push us on our fashion sense, give us relationship advice, and scrutinise everyone who shows an interest in us. But when it comes to what really matters, there is nobody you are accountable to spiritually. That has to change. Get accountable.

5. STRUCTURE

Whatever you don't build a structure around will not thrive. If you don't have a to-do list, you're most likely not going to get anything done. So, rather than saying, "I will pray today," Have a specific time and make it consistent. For example, in our church, we have four prayer times: 6 a.m., noon, 8 p.m., and 2 a.m. You cannot say you're busy round the clock, that you cannot spend even 15 minutes to pray at noon. That's a problem!

So, draw up a plan for yourself and stick to it. What time will you pray? For how long? What time will you study your Bible? For how long? Do it now.

CHAPTER FOURTEEN
A FINAL GUIDE TO PRAYER

x x x x x x x x

As a final note, I would like to re-emphasise that prayer can be learnt. Some are of the opinion that spiritual things cannot be taught but are instead spontaneous. At times, when we see people who function well in the things of the Spirit, we subconsciously conclude that they see what they are seeing because they have special gifts. And by so doing, we exempt ourselves from the responsibility of learning to see what they see and do what they do.

Again, when the disciples said to Jesus:, "Teach us to pray." Jesus didn't say no to the disciples' request. He didn't say "The things of the Spirit are mysterious," rather He taught them to pray. All the chapters in this book were written with one purpose in mind:

to teach you to pray. Do well to apply them. Here are seven key tips to remember:

1. **LEARN TO PRAY HEARTFELT PRAYERS**

    There must be an emotional investment in your prayer. Like **James 5:16b** says, *"The heartfelt continued prayer of a righteous man makes tremendous power available."* Here are tips to help you pray heartfelt prayers:

    a. **Meditate on the Word:** The Word of God and prayer have a symbiotic relationship; this is why sometimes, it's good to warm your heart with the Word before praying. Meditating on the Word before you pray gives your heart something to focus on, making it easier for your prayer to be heartfelt. To meditate means to focus one's mind on something for a period of time. In a more descriptive term, it means to caress a thought all over the walls of your mind for a sustained period of time until it becomes your predominant thought. This is what meditating on God's Word does to you. It helps you zero in your focus on God as you pray.

    b. **Put away distractions:** If you want to pray heartfelt prayers, you must put away things that try to take your attention. People nowadays struggle to pray for long

A FINAL GUIDE TO PRAYER

periods of time without being tempted to check their phones to see what they are missing out on. However, one with a divided attention in the place of prayer will not be able to pray heartfelt prayers.

1. DEVOTE TIME

It must be said that this is not something extra religious people do, it's a spiritual phenomenon. You cannot master what you've not spent time practising. James did not describe the effective prayer of the righteous man as being "heartfelt" alone, it must also be "continued." The more time you give to prayer, the better you get at it. Come to think of it, if prayer is communication with God, and you claim to love God, shouldn't you be eager to spend more time with Him? Besides, the practise of spending time in prayer is something we find in the Bible as well; there are too many examples to be ignored. This was the culture of Jesus.

"Now it came to pass in those days that He went out to the mountain to pray, and continued all night in prayer to God."

(Luke 6:12)

This was also the culture of the apostles. In Acts 13, the prophets and teachers in the church in Antioch met to pray and fast. The fast being mentioned goes to show that the meeting must have lasted a couple of hours, at least six hours.

> *"As they ministered to the Lord and fasted, the Holy Spirit said, "Now separate to Me Barnabas and Saul for the work to which I have called them." Then, having fasted and prayed, and laid hands on them, they sent them away."*
> **(Acts 13:2-3)**

The culture of spending time in prayer is a skill you must learn because you will need it. Learn to build muscle in the place of prayer now. This is the idea—just like you must be consistent in the gym to be fit, regardless of how much you do in one day, you must also do the same with prayer. Prayer must be a lifestyle. You have not yet learnt to pray until you learn to pray without ceasing. It's better to pray shorter prayers consistently than to pray long occasionally.

Learning to spend longer time in the place of prayer won't happen suddenly; you would have to grow into it with consistency. For example, you can start with 15 minutes of prayer daily, then make it twice a day, then three times a day, and then you increase the time from 15 to 20 minutes. Before you know it, you'd have been praying for an hour every day, consistently. Now, as time goes by, you can keep increasing the time. That is how to build a culture of spending time in prayer.

2. CREATE AN ENVIRONMENT OF CONSTANT POSITIVE PROVOCATION

One very simple way to keep a fervent prayer life is to be intentional about the influences you allow around you. A good example of this we see with Saul in 1 Samuel 10:11-12:

> *"When they came there to the hill, there was a group of prophets to meet him; then the Spirit of God came upon him, and he prophesied among them. And it happened, when all who knew him formerly saw that he indeed prophesied among the prophets, that the people said to one another, 'What is this that has come upon the son of Kish? Is Saul also among the prophets?'"*

Saul had yet to prophesy prior to this moment; however, being in the company of prophets changed that. It's the same when it comes to devotional fervour. The influence you allow around you matters. Someone else's spiritual fervour can provoke your own, just like a jumpstart cable. If your vehicle is not moving, someone can jumpstart you. I believe this is the most important thing you can do in your walk with God. This is why God doesn't want us to be alone; it is so members of the Body can edify one another.

> *"Let us consider one another to provoke unto love and to good works, not forsaking the assembling of ourselves together, as is the manner of some, but exhorting one another, and so much the more as you see the Day approaching."*
> **(Hebrews 10:24-25)**

This is why the gathering of the saints is so important. God doesn't want us to be alone, He wants a body that edifies itself. He wants us to provoke one another to do better when it comes to our devotional life. You're more impressionable than you think, so learn to feed off the energy of other people. Let their walk with God bless you and spur you to do better. The mindset is that every day, you must keep seeing something that encourages you in your spiritual walk.

Another way you can create an atmosphere of positive provocation is by playing songs that will stir you up to pray,

A FINAL GUIDE TO PRAYER

or sermons that talk about prayer, or consecration to God. Even if you are engaged in other activities, just leave it playing in the background. If you do this frequently, you are more likely to pray frequently.

3. SINGING

This is a very vital aspect of prayer that many either don't pay enough attention to, or have despised. Many of the songs we sing are prayers, but we despise them because they have a melody. Whatever you are struggling to utter as a prayer, you can sing. Get songs with lyrics that align with what you want to pray about; play them and sing along.

4. BE RELIGIOUS ABOUT THE TIME

It is important to have a time when you pray; it is a biblical principle. The apostles had this:

> "Now Peter and John went up together to the temple at the hour of prayer, the ninth hour."
>
> **- Acts 3:1**

> "The next day, as they went on their journey and drew near the city, Peter went up on the housetop to pray, about the sixth hour."
>
> **- Acts 10:9**

Decide what time you will pray and for how long, then stick to it religiously. Have you noticed that your prayer life began to dwindle when you convinced yourself that it wasn't about the time? This is because having a structure is what will birth consistency, not relying on your willpower or feeling of being motivated. You are not smarter than Jesus and the apostles. If they had a structure to their prayers, you must, too.

5. HAVE A PRAYER PARTNER

It is important that, in the church, we have a system of accountability. This is particularly important for those who are currently struggling with being consistent with their prayer times. Even if you aren't currently struggling, having a prayer partner helps you do even better. Again, it is important to note that in the scripture quoted earlier (Acts 3:1), it was Peter and John going to pray together. We must have such relationships today as well. Have people you are known to pray with.

6. TRIUMPH30 DEVOTIONAL

On a final note, the Triumph30 Devotional is a tool you want to take advantage of. It is so crucial that you can tune in four times a day and have someone lead you in a time of prayer. Search Triumph30 Live on YouTube to join today.

A FINAL GUIDE TO PRAYER

Finally, my team has compiled an album of prayers and confessions to get you started on your prayer journey.